THE BEATLES ON VINYL

The Must Have Records For Your Collection

Written by Pete Chrisp

sona BOOKS

sona BOOKS

© Danann Media Publishing Limited 2021

First published in the UK 2021 by Sona Books an imprint of Danann Media Publishing Ltd.

WARNING: For private domestic use only, any unauthorised copying, hiring, lending or public performance of this book is illegal.

CAT NO: SON0490

Photography courtesy of

Getty images:

- LMPC
- Mark and Colleen Hayward
- Movie Poster Image Art
- Santi Visalli
- Michael Ochs Archives

- Arthur Steel/Mirrorpix
- Daily Herald/Mirrorpix
- Healey/Mirrorpix
- Cummings Archives/Redferns
- Bettmann

- GAB Archive/Redferns
- RB/Redferns
- David Redfern/Redferns
- Roger Viollet Collection

Alamy:

- PA Images
- IMAGEPAST
- Patti McConville / Stockimo

- CBW
- Jeffrey Blackler
- Rajko Simunovic

- Sueddeutsche Zeitung Photo

Endpapers: nick-fewings/Unsplash
Other Unsplash images: friso-baaij

Other Images Courtesy of Wiki Commons

Book layout & design Darren Grice at Ctrl-d

All rights reserved. No Part of this title may be reproduced or transmitted in any material form (including photocopying or storing it in any medium by electronic means and whether or not transiently or incidentally to some other use of this publication) without the written permission of the copyright owner, except in accordance with the provisions of the Copyright, Designs and Patents Act 1988.Applications for the copyright owner's written permission should be addressed to the publisher.

This is an independent publication and it is unofficial and unauthorised and as such has no connection with the artist or artists featured, their management or any other organisation connected in any way whatsoever with the artist or artists featured in the book.

Made in EU.
ISBN: 978-1-912918-57-7

Contents

INTRODUCTION	8
STUDIO ALBUMS	12
LIVE ALBUMS	82
COMPILATION ALBUMS	92
BOXSETS	106
SINGLES	114
EPs	136
BEATLES TOP 20 ALBUMS	144
ACKNOWLEDGEMENTS AND SOURCES	146

INTRODUCTION

"I always thought they were going to be pretty big."

Brian Epstein

The Beatles. Never underestimate the Beatles. They're the greatest band of all time. But they're much more important than that.

These four exceptional young men gelled perfectly to create a band far greater than the sum of their considerable talents and personalities. Right from the start, from their very first album in 1963, they were way ahead of the game. Every record they made was the best so far and immediately became a band-imposed benchmark. The next one had to be even better, and almost always was. As for the songs: originality, diversity, emotion, perception, energy, humour, lyricism, melodies and harmonies… no two Beatles songs were ever quite the same, but almost always profoundly enduring.

Leave it to Sir George Martin, who produced the original Beatles albums back in the Sixties, to quantify the importance and standing of the official Beatles' canon in music history:

"The best songwriters of our generation, of our time. They were comparable to Cole Porter or George Gershwin or Jerome Kern, any of the great American songwriters of the Thirties. Their music will be heard in 50 years' time, if not longer."

The English lyricist, Sir Tim Rice, aims higher still: "The Beatles were the Mozart of popular music. No-one ever equaled their extraordinary output between 1963 and 1970."

During those seven years, the Beatles changed everything. When *Sgt. Pepper's Lonely Hearts Club Band* arrived in '67, every pop and rock musician in the world realised that the game had changed; anything was possible but they had to catch up. Without the Beatles, many of the biggest bands of the Seventies and beyond would never have existed. Sounds pompous, but that's how important and influential the Beatles were, and still are.

It's now almost 60 years since their first album was released. Their entire back catalogue will continue to be enjoyed and appreciated for many more years to come but, sadly, there can never be any more Beatles records. The good news is that there's never been a better time to listen to them in the way they were meant to be heard: vinyl, on a decent record player through decent speakers. If you've never heard a Beatles album before, you're a lucky person. Start now. Play them all. Turn off your mind, relax and float downstream.

Pete Chrisp

May 2021

INTRODUCTION

With
THE BEATLES AT
...Peppers...
A Hard Day
...ATLES   LET IT
...VOLVER - The Bea
Please Me —

The Beatles

THE HOLLYWOOD

s Night — Th

the Beatles

STUDIO ALBUMS

Please note: track listings throughout the book are composed by Lennon-McCartney unless stated otherwise.

"The recording is not what one hears, but what one must make others hear."

Sir George Martin CBE

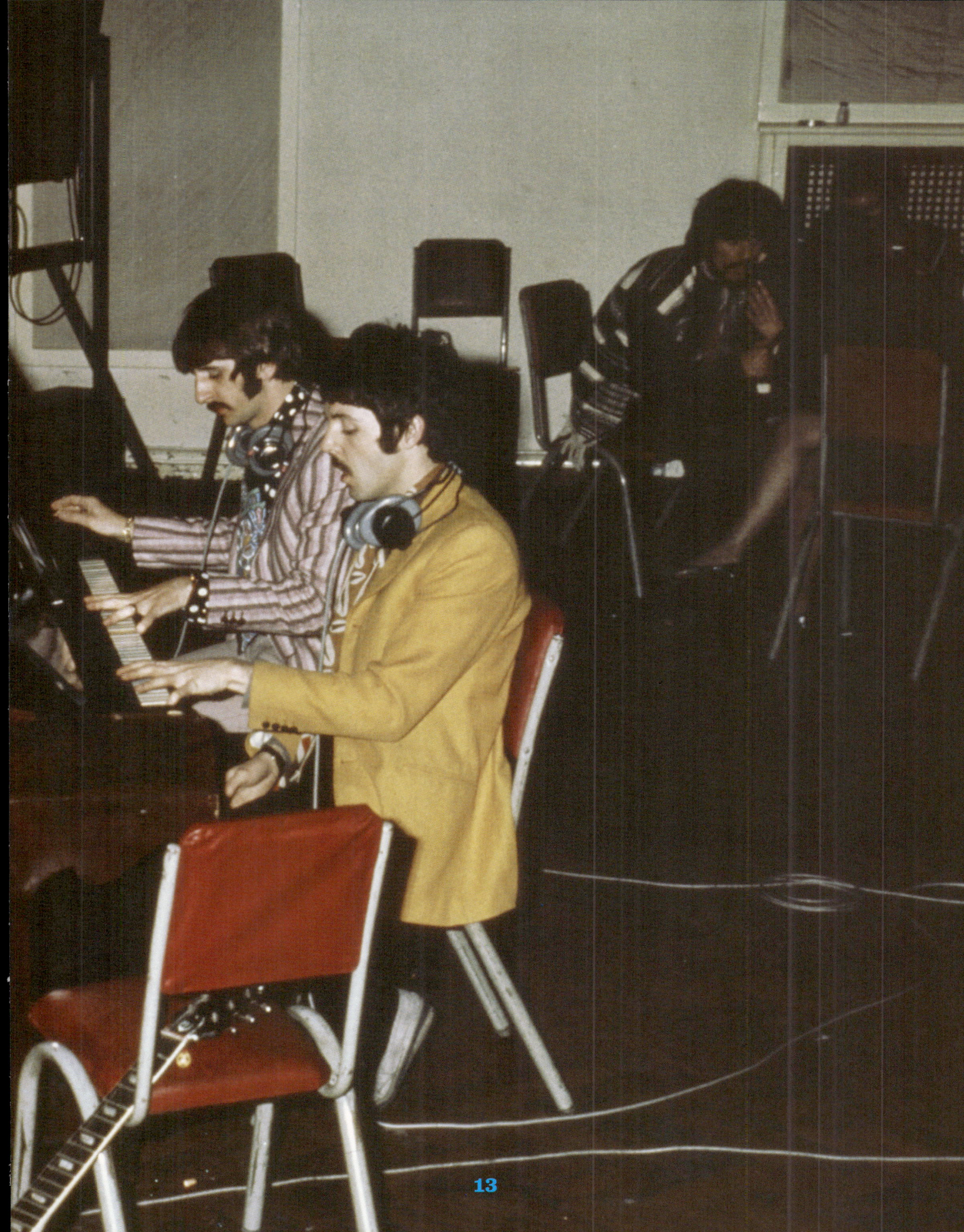

PLEASE PLEASE ME

Released:	**22 November 1963**
Label:	**Parlophone**
Producer:	**George Martin**
Recorded:	**EMI Studios, London**
UK:	**No.1**
USA:	**Not Released**

STUDIO ALBUMS

Side 1:
1. I Saw Her Standing There
2. Misery
3. Anna (Go to Him) (Alexander)
4. Chains (Goffin-King)
5. Boys (Dixon-Farrell)
6. Ask Me Why
7. Please Please Me

Side 2:
1. Love Me Do
2. P.S. I Love You
3. Baby it's You (David-Williams-Bacharach)
4. Do You Want to Know a Secret
5. A Taste of Honey (Scott-Marlow)
6. There's a Place
7. Twist and Shout (Medley-Russell)

Never has a debut album from a British band ever been as important, as memorable, as remarkable or as purely enjoyable as the Beatles' *Please Please Me*. Recorded in little more than 13 hours on 11 February 1963 at EMI Studios in London following the success of their first two hit singles, 'Love Me Do' and 'Please Please Me' (reaching Nos. 17 and 2 on the UK's Official Charts), here was a new, young band clearly going somewhere fast. For Parlophone, it was the perfect time to take advantage of their phenomenal rise and produce their debut album.

Their producer, George Martin – a decidedly posh, ex-Royal Navy man known for his comedy records with the likes of Peter Sellers, Bernard Cribbens, Peter Cook and Dudley Moore – hadn't been too impressed by the Beatles when he met them for the first time, apart from appreciating their lively personalities and humorous chat. Quite appropriate, really. But he'd decided to give them a go at EMI and admitted to being pleasantly surprised by the quality of their first two singles. The question was, could they maintain that standard for their first album – especially given that only 12 hours recording time had been allocated at EMI's Studio 2.

It wasn't a great start when the Beatles arrived at Abbey Road that morning all suffering from nasty colds, especially John Lennon. Of the 10 songs to be recorded that day, Lennon was due to sing lead vocals on five of them, plus backing vocals on the others.

As producer it was George Martin's responsibility to choose the running order for the recording and for the album's track listing. Sensibly he decided to leave 'Twist and Shout' until last, knowing its vocals would require a throat-ripping performance, especially from a man swallowing pints of milk and Zubes throat lozenges to ease the pain.

Instead, they kicked off with the gentle ballad 'There's a Place', one of eight songs from the 14 that would be Lennon-McCartney compositions – unprecedented for a pop group at that time. Four songs had proved their popularity already as the A- and B-sides of their first two Top 20 hits. What else did they have to offer? George Martin needed to know: "I asked them what they had which we could record quickly and the

THE BEATLES ON VINYL

answer was, their stage act."

Since 2 January the Beatles had been travelling up and down the UK every day, largely performing as part of Helen Shapiro's package tour. This was a band as tight as any band could be, and the answer to George's question was in their next recording, 'I Saw Her Standing There', which opens the album.

"I taught them the importance of the hook," said George. "You had to get people's attention in the first 10 seconds…" He wasn't disappointed. Paul McCartney's opening "1, 2, 3, 4," is the countdown to a recorded sound and songwriting prowess with which no other band could compete over the next seven years and beyond.

"Well she was just seventeen
You know what I mean…
And the way she looked
Was way beyond compare…"

George Martin had achieved what he had wanted – to represent the Beatles' authentic live sound at the Cavern Club in Liverpool, where the seeds of their reputation had been sown. Initially he'd considered recording the album there, but decided it was safer to book EMI Studios for what would, in essence, be a live performance. Ten tracks, one after the other, representing bluesy ballads, soul, R&B, Motown, and straight rock 'n' roll, all performed and recorded superbly, with the addition of their first two hit singles and B-sides that had been recorded in pretty

INTRODUCING… THE BEATLES

Released: 10 January 1964
Label: Vee-Jay
UK: Not released
USA: No. 2

Side 1:
1. I Saw Her Standing There
2. Misery
3. Anna (Go to Him) (Alexander)
4. Chains (Goffin-King)
5. Boys (Dixon-Farrell)
6. Love Me Do (Replaced by 'Ask Me Why' in February 1964)

Side 2:
1. P.S. I Love You (Replaced by 'Please Please Me' in February 1964)
2. Baby it's You (David-Williams-Bacharach)
3. Do You Want to Know a Secret
4. A Taste of Honey (Scott-Marlow)
5. There's a Place
6. Twist and Shout (Medley-Russell)

STUDIO ALBUMS

much the same way a few weeks earlier. Apart from some minor keyboard overdubs added by George Martin to 'Misery' and 'Baby it's You' a few days later, that was that. When the time had come for Lennon to have a go at the LP's final track, 'Twist and Shout' he nailed it on the first take, despite singing with a sandpapered throat.

Said George Martin: "I don't know how they do it. We've been recording all day but the longer we go on the better they get."

The whole day's session had cost approximately £400 (equivalent to about £9,000 today) – the best investment EMI ever made. The respected theatre photographer, Angus McBean, knocked out the cover photography equally urgently at EMI's London HQ in Manchester Square.

On the LP's rear sleeve notes, music journalist Tony Barrow (soon to become the Beatles' press officer and the man who first coined the phrase, 'the Fab Four'), said: "I have never seen a British group leap to the forefront of the scene with such speed and energy."

After recording Please Please Me, the Beatles headed off the next day to perform two gigs in Sheffield and Oldham. They played live virtually every day from then on until recording their next two singles and, in July, their second album. There were the answers to Barrow's incomprehension. Sheer hard work.

Please Please Me was released on 22 March 1963 and hit the top of the UK album charts in May, knocking off Cliff Richard and the Shadows' *Summer Holiday*. It remained there for 30 weeks before being replaced by … their new LP, *With the Beatles*.

ABOVE: *The Beatles arrive at Kennedy Airport for the first time from London for a 10-day tour, February 7, 1964*

THE EARLY BEATLES

Released:	**22 March 1965**
Label:	**Capitol**
UK:	**Not Released**
USA:	**No. 43**

STUDIO ALBUMS

Side 1:
1. Love Me Do
2. **Twist and Shout** (Medley-Russell)
3. **Anna (Go to Him)** (Alexander)
4. **Chains** (Goffin-King)
5. **Boys** (Dixon-Farrell)
6. Ask Me Why

Side 2:
1. Please Please Me
2. P.S. I Love You
3. **Baby it's You** (David-Williams-Bacharach)
4. **A Taste of Honey** (Scott-Marlow)
5. Do You Want to Know a Secret

It seems hard to believe that, when the Beatles' first two singles were released in the UK in 1963, they were both turned down by EMI's American subsidiary Capitol because they were considered inappropriate for the US market.

George Martin and the Beatles' manager, Brian Epstein, were far from happy and decided to offer it elsewhere. With the help of the New York licensing agency, Transglobal Music, EMI handed over the two singles to a small Chicago-based record company, Vee-Jay, plus the rights to the *Please Please Me* LP as part of a five-year, first-refusal deal.

Vee-Jay couldn't believe their luck and intended to release the complete album in July '63, but financial issues forced them to delay it until January '64. By that time they'd also decided to stick to the US norm of just 12 tracks on an LP, dropping 'Please Please Me' and 'Ask Me Why'. They also removed McCartney's '1-2-3-4' from the opening of 'I Saw Her Standing There'. It was America's opening salvo in its approach to meddle with Beatles' albums running orders willy-nilly, and usually for the worse.

It also signaled a legal battle with Capitol who had realised their error and released their first LP, *Meet the Beatles*, just 10 days after *Introducing... the Beatles*, taking it straight to No. 1. Vee-Jay's offering sat at No. 2 for nine weeks. Not bad for 'inappropriate' British rock 'n' roll.

It all gets a bit difficult here but it transpired that Capitol already owned the rights to the Beatles' first single 'Love Me Do'/'P.S. I Love You' and took out an injunction just six days after *Introducing... the Beatles* was launched, forcing Vee-Jay to release a revised version with those two tracks replaced by the two that had originally been dropped. With the case settled in April '64, using various different names and track listings, Vee-Jay had been able to release four different LPs, five singles and an EP from those tracks, selling millions during the 15 months from July '63 until their licence expired in October '64.

Once Vee-Jay were out of the way, Capitol eventually and rather sheepishly released in March '65 what was virtually the album they had turned down in 1963, entitled *The Early Beatles*. Just three tracks less. And a different running order. Obviously. In truth, all US Beatles albums up to and including *Revolver* are compilations in one way or another.

WITH THE BEATLES

Released:	**22 November 1963**
Label:	**Parlophone**
Producer:	**George Martin**
Recorded:	**EMI Studios, London**
UK:	**No.1**
USA:	**Not Released**

STUDIO ALBUMS

Side 1:
1. It Won't Be Long
2. All I've Got to Do
3. All My Loving
4. Don't Bother Me (Harrison)
5. Little Child
6. Till There Was You (Willson)
7. Please Mr. Postman
(Holland-Bateman-Garrett-Dobbins-Gorman)

Side 2:
1. Roll Over Beethoven (Berry)
2. Hold Me Tight
3. You Really Got a Hold on Me (Robinson)
4. I Wanna Be Your Man
5. Devil in Her Heart (Drapkin)
6. Not a Second Time
7. Money (That's What I Want) (Bradford-Gordy)

By November 1963, 'Beatlemania' – a term invented by the British press – was up and running, and not just among hordes of screaming teenage girls. The band's punishing itinerary of live shows combined with radio and TV broadcasts, highlighted by their Royal Variety Performance at London's Prince of Wales Theatre (where John famously asked those in the cheap seats to clap, the rest to rattle their jewellery) had seen the band elevated to the status of national treasures. The royal family loved them, while among more serious establishment critics, their songwriting skills had been compared to the likes of Mozart and Mahler.

Their second UK album, *With the Beatles*, arrived eight months after *Please Please Me* to satisfy the UK's baying fans with another collection of eight Beatles-penned tracks – seven from Lennon-McCartney and the first from George Harrison – plus six cover versions, all of which had proved popular with live audiences.

The two latest Beatles singles 'She Loves You' and 'I Want to Hold Your Hand' had both received record-breaking advanced orders – over 500,000 and a million copies respectively. Although album sales in the UK generally didn't compare with singles in the Sixties, *With the Beatles* followed the same path to success and, by 1 November '63, had received advanced orders of more than a quarter of a million copies – an all-time British record. It went straight to No. 1 in the albums charts, remaining there for 21 weeks, and even managed to make it to No. 11 in the singles charts where all sales were taken into account at that time, whatever the format. By Christmas they had sold half a million. By September 1965, it became the first UK LP to achieve a million sales. British sales records tumbled like 10-pins. Still it ranks as the Beatles' third best-selling UK album.

Was it, is it, really that good? Recorded between July and October 1963 over seven separate days, *With the Beatles* certainly provided them with much more studio time compared to their debut LP, but

BELOW: *The Beatles in Stockholm 1963*

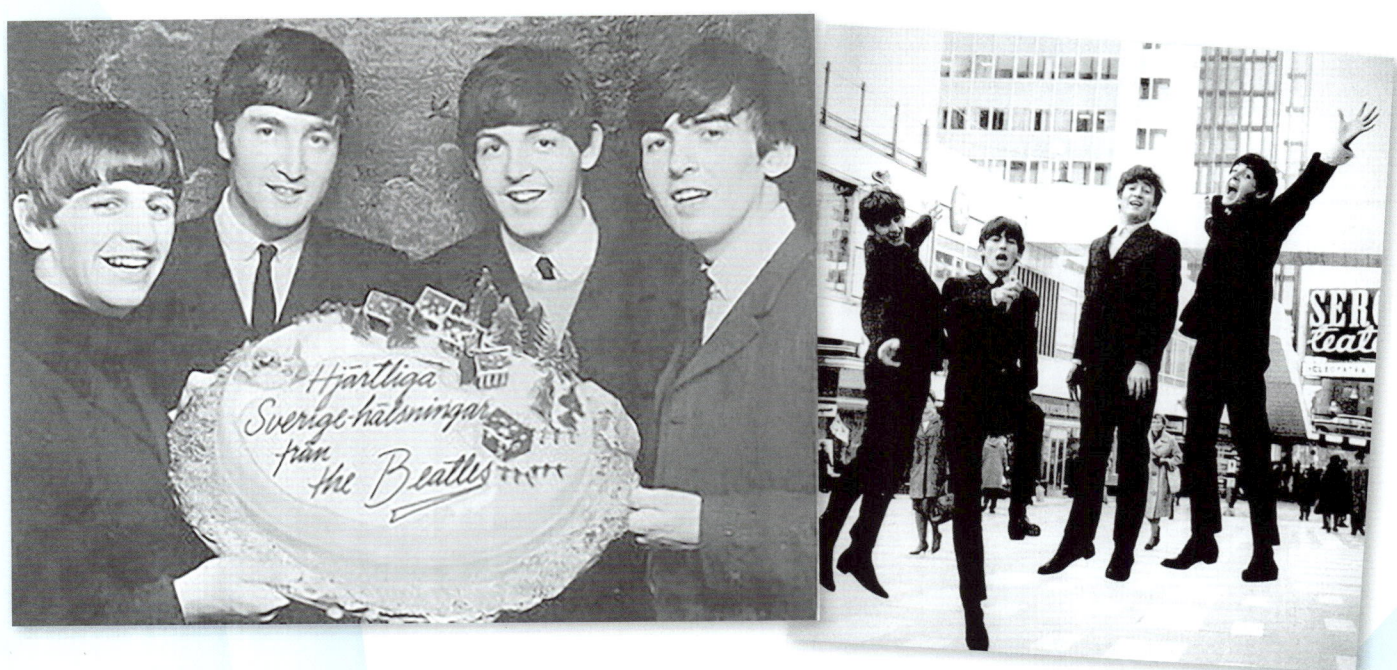

they were still under immense pressure to come up with eight more tracks to add to the six covers they had concentrated on first. The new songs, of course, arrived on time, but there are some who feel that the album would have been even better if they'd included their two current hit singles in preference to some of the others.

In *The Beatles Anthology* George Martin acknowledged such feelings when he commented: "The first album was really a recital of their repertoire. We weren't thinking in terms of an album being an entity in itself back then. We would record singles, and the ones that weren't issued as singles would be put onto an album – which is how the second album, *With the Beatles*, was put together. It was just a collection of their songs, and one or two other people's songs as well."

There had been more input from the band, with the six covers, as Tony Barrow described in his sleeve notes as being, "a batch of 'personal choice' pieces selected from the recorded repertoires of the American R&B artists they admire most". Notably three Motown numbers ('Please Mr. Postman' by the Marvellettes, 'You Really Got a Hold On Me' by Smokey Robinson and the Miracles, and 'Money [That's What I Want]' by Barrett Strong); 'Devil in Her Heart' by the Donays; 'Roll Over Beethoven' by Chuck Berry; and 'Till There Was You', a lovely ballad from the successful musical, *The Music Man*, which had been sung by Sue Raney, Peggy Lee and (in the 1962 movie) Shirley Jones, among many others. All great songs by performers they loved, but could they have filled the gaps any better?

Either way, *With the Beatles* gets underway in the same vein as *Please Please Me* with a rip-roaring opener, 'It Won't Be Long' sung, this time, by John. It's followed by a run of four more Beatles tracks including Harrison's country-and-western-influenced 'Don't Bother Me'.

STUDIO ALBUMS

Four of the seven tracks on Side 2 are covers, interspersed with the remaining three Lennon-McCartney numbers, including Ringo singing 'I Wanna Be Your Man' with the same energy he'd delivered on 'Boys' for the debut album.

There was more input and musical influence from the four band members whose depth of musical knowledge had been underestimated by many. They knew their stuff and they knew what worked well. George Martin's important input was more in terms of his arrangements and recording skills, plus his keyboard overdubs. He didn't write, or pick, the songs; the Beatles were growing up fast.

And visually, there was no doubt that they had progressed considerably. For the first time they expressed an interest in being involved in the cover artwork and asked Robert Freeman (a photographer renowned for his black and white images of jazz musicians) to base his cover photography on earlier shots taken by Astrid Kirchherr (a German photographer and fiancé of the Beatles' original bass player, Stuart Sutcliffe) during their time in Hamburg.

In Freeman's superb, grainy front cover image, gone are the quiffs and any semblance of gawkiness. Instead stood the Beatles in half-shadows, black tops, new haircuts, looking mean and moody. The message was clear: If you want it, here it is, come and get it.

Millions did.

BELOW LEFT: *The Beatles and Swedish singer Lill-Babs 1963*
BELOW RIGHT: *Taken outside the Birmingham Hippodrome in 1963 when the Beatles were smuggled into the venue in the back of a police van*

MEET THE BEATLES

Released:	**20 January 1964**
Label:	**Capitol**
UK:	**Not Released**
USA:	**No. 1**

STUDIO ALBUMS

Side 1:
1. I Want to Hold Your Hand
2. I Saw Her Standing There
3. This Boy
4. It Won't Be Long
5. All I've Got to Do
6. All My Loving

Side 2:
1. Don't Bother Me (Harrison)
2. Little Child
3. Till There Was You (Willson)
4. Hold Me Tight
5. I Wanna Be Your Man
6. Not a Second Time

64

For once, there are many who think the US version of the Beatles' second UK album, closely entitled *Meet the Beatles*, offered a better song line-up than *With the Beatles*. You can see their point. Capitol understandably wanted to launch them with the huge hit that broke them in the USA, 'I Want to Hold Your Hand' as an opener, followed by its two B-sides, 'I Saw Her Standing There' in the USA and 'This Boy' in the UK. From that point on it's the eight Beatles tracks from *With the Beatles* but dropping all but one of the cover versions, 'Till There Was You'. At least they did keep Robert Freeman's great cover portrait, but for some reason gave it a blue tint…

By the middle of February *Meet the Beatles* topped the US charts and stayed there for 11 weeks until the next Capitol Beatles release arrived, the snappily titled *The Beatles' Second Album*. After their initial delays, Capitol was trying its best to catch up, but Messrs. Lennon and McCartney were knocking out hits too frequently.

ABOVE: *The Beatles Take on America, 1964*

A HARD DAY'S NIGHT

Released:	**10 July 1964**
Label:	**Parlophone**
Producer:	**George Martin**
Recorded:	**EMI Studios, London and Pathé Marconi Studios, Paris**
UK:	**No.1**
USA:	**Own version released**

Side 1:
1. A Hard Day's Night
2. I Should Have Known Better
3. If I Fell
4. I'm Happy Just to Dance With You
5. And I Love Her
6. Tell Me Why
7. Can't Buy Me Love

Side 2:
1. Any Time at All
2. I'll Cry Instead
3. Things We Said Today
4. When I Get Home
5. You Can't Do That
6. I'll Be Back

What a difference 15 months can make when you've been "working like a dog". And they certainly had. This, just their third UK album, is remarkable on so many different levels.

First, and most obvious, for the first time all 13 songs were written by John Lennon and Paul McCartney. No covers. No standards. Only one track ('I'm Happy Just to Dance with You') was co-written; Lennon primarily wrote nine of the 13 tracks on the album, while McCartney's own contributions – 'And I Love Her' (a ballad for his girlfriend, the actress Jane Asher), the folky 'Things We Said Today' and the superb movie-closing 'Can't Buy Me Love' – sat, despite their brilliance, in the shadow of Lennon's nine; this was his album and he had demonstrated unequivocally his ability to produce great songs out of a top hat whenever needed, and especially when needed urgently.

Secondly, the album was put together primarily as the soundtrack for the film of the same name – the first of its kind. Here was a pop music comedy film that was actually well-acted, very funny, and received with open arms by the public, the media and the film industry. Both George Martin (for the music score) and writer Alun Owen (for the screenplay) were nominated for Oscars, while the four Beatles were nominated for BAFTAS for 'most promising newcomer to leading film roles'. All they had done was be themselves but, in a matter of just a few months, had managed to write the theme tune, sing the theme tune, make the film, be the film stars etc etc.

Elvis Presley must have been spitting feathers having to sit through the movie and listen to the soundtrack: not only had the Beatles stolen his pop crown, here was a great film, great songs, great script, great director, great actors. Elvis's effort that same year had been the movie *Viva Las Vegas*; watchable, but not a patch on *A Hard Day's Night*.

Only the first side of the album contained the titles from the film soundtrack, while Side 2 offered six more songs written for (but not actually included in) the movie. Either way, this was 'new pop'. With its raw aggression combined with perfect harmonies, clanging 12-string electric guitars and that inexplicable but unforgettable opening chord,

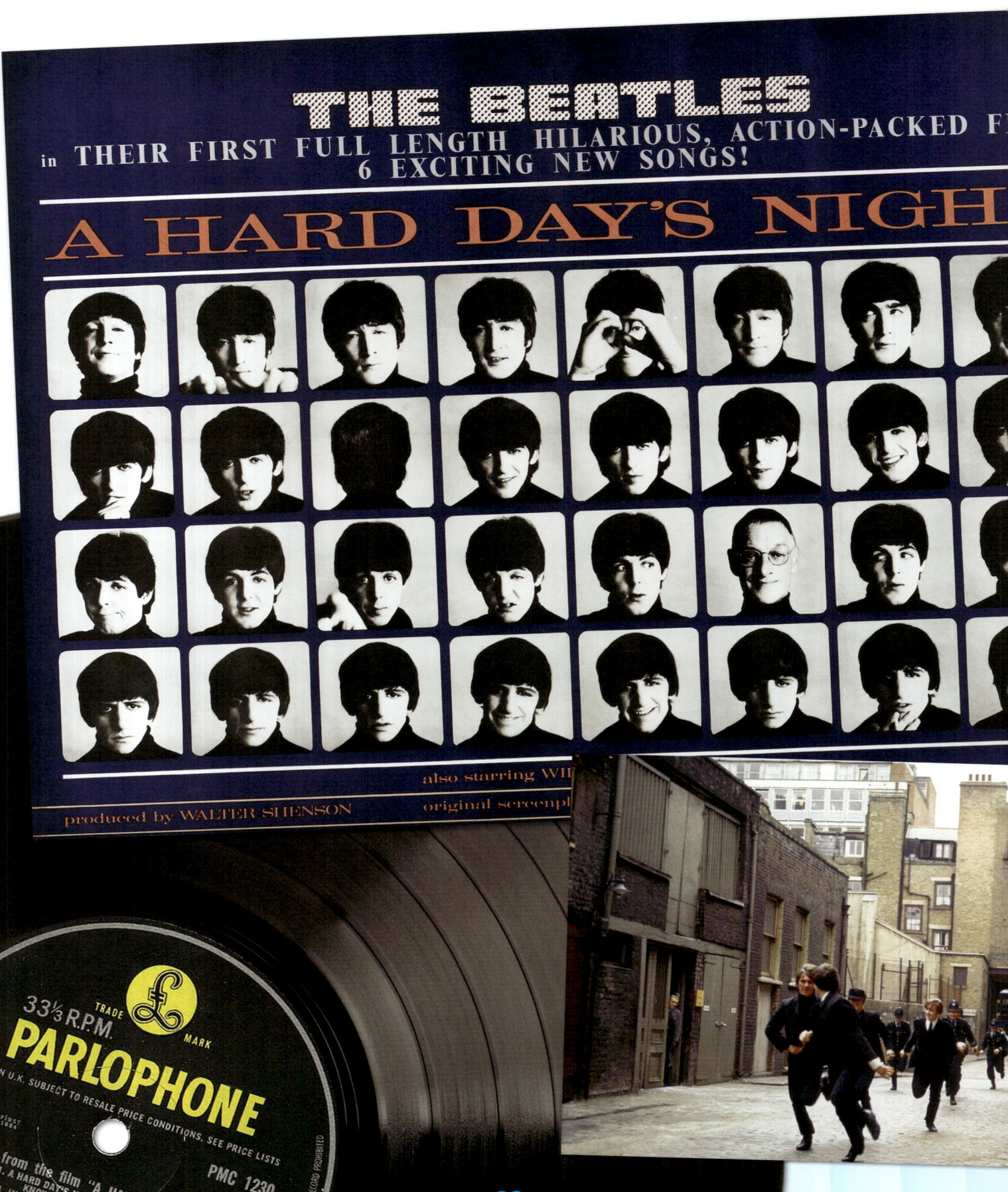

STUDIO ALBUMS

here was the Beatles' (and especially John's) most impressive work so far. Just on its own the album sounded brilliant, but combine Side 1 with the sheer excitement of the slapstick, Marx Brothers-esque, black and white movie images… this was nothing short of a masterpiece.

It is true that there's something of a lack of input from George and Ringo as far as the soundtrack is concerned, other than their instrumental talents and Harrison taking lead vocals on the Lennon-McCartney track "I'm Happy Just to Dance With You', but their comedic acting skills in the film stand out and signpost their genuine interest and involvement in movie-making in later years. It was Ringo, of course, who had come up with the film/album title when he once uttered, off the cuff, that a studio session had been "a hard day's night". John Lennon found it amusing and included the phrase in his prose and verse book *In His Own Write*, which film director Dick Lester happened to read. He proclaimed it the perfect title for the movie and soundtrack album. He was absolutely right. Everything just fell into place.

A Hard Day's Night was released on 10 July 1964, four days after the film premiered in London in front of Princess Margaret, and shot straight to No. 1, where it stayed for five months. Artistic praise and awards nominations were handed out like confetti at a wedding and the cash came rolling in. Meanwhile, the Beatles – now the biggest stars in the world – climbed back onto the moneymaking treadmill, despite their obvious signs of exhaustion. Within a month they were back at Abbey Road working on their next album and preparing to leave for their first proper US tour.

LEFT: *The British poster and still from the film A Hard Day's Night, 1964*

A HARD DAY'S NIGHT

Released: **26 June 1964**
Label: **United Artists Records**
UK: **Own version released**
USA: **No. 1**

Side 1:
1. A Hard Day's Night
2. Tell Me Why
3. I'll Cry Instead
4. I Should Have Known Better
5. I'm Happy Just to Dance With You
6. And I Love Her

Side 2:
1. I Should Have Known Better (instrumental)
2. If I Fell
3. And I Love Her (instrumental)
4. Ringo's Theme (This Boy) (instrumental)
5. Can't Buy Me Love
6. A Hard Day's Night (instrumental)

SOMETHING NEW

Released:	**20 July 1964**
Label:	**Capitol**
UK:	**Not Released**
USA:	**No. 2**

Side 1:
1. I'll Cry Instead
2. Things We Said Today
3. Any Time at All
4. When I Get Home
5. Slow Down (Williams)
6. Matchbox (Perkins)

Side 2:
1. Tell Me Why
2. And I Love Her
3. I'm Happy Just to Dance With You
4. If I Fell
5. Komm, Gib Mir Deine Hand
(German version of 'I Want to Hold Your Hand')

Equally bizarre from Capitol in its attempts to catch up with the Beatles' album output was the decision to release *Something New*, a very similar LP to United Artist's release of *A Hard Day's Night* that had been launched just over three weeks before – two weeks before the UK version. Capitol didn't release *A Hard Day's Night* because they did not have the rights to release Beatles film scores, but in 1980 EMI acquired United Artists Records and reissued the album on Capitol.

UA's version of the soundtrack was rather unusual as well. All seven songs from the film were featured, along with 'I'll Cry Instead', but also included four instrumental versions of Lennon and McCartney songs arranged by George Martin and performed by an orchestra of studio musicians. These might not have been too popular with many young Beatles fans in the USA (it does sound suspiciously like something you've borrowed from mom and dad's cheesy record collection) but if you like Sixties jazz-influenced, Henry Mancini-style soundtracks, you'll love them. Martin's arrangements are superb.

Something New, on the other hand, was Capitol's attempt to compete with UA's release and, once again, is more of a compilation than a soundtrack. Only four of the songs from the movie are included on Side 2, which then concludes with a German language version of 'I Want to Hold Your Hand'. Interesting.

Side 1 omits the movie's title song but includes four other tracks from the UK album (only one of which is on the US version), plus two covers from the *Long Tall Sally* EP. Confused? Join the club. Probably best to stick with the UK album.

BEATLES FOR SALE

Released:	**4 December 1964**
Label:	**Parlophone**
Producer:	**George Martin**
Recorded:	**EMI Studios, London**
UK:	**No.1**
USA:	**Own version released**

STUDIO ALBUMS

Side 1:
1. No Reply
2. I'm a Loser
3. Baby's in Black
4. Rock and Roll Music (Berry)
5. I'll Follow the Sun
6. Mr. Moonlight (Johnson)
7. Kansas City/Hey-Hey-Hey-Hey (Leiber-Stoller/Penniman)

Side 2:
1. Eight Days a Week
2. Words of Love (Holly)
3. Honey Don't (Perkins)
4. Every Little Thing
5. I Don't Want to Spoil the Party
6. What You're Doing
7. Everybody's Trying to Be My Baby (Perkins)

Beatles for Sale, plain and simple, is the Beatles' country-and-western album, and a pretty good one at that. Having spent June to September 1964 touring the world, particularly the USA, the Beatles had become worldwide superstars but were running out of steam when it came to writing new material. Only eight of the tracks on Beatles for Sale are original songs, the other six being covers including two Carl Perkins numbers that reflected the band's love of rockabilly music – an early form of rock 'n' roll that combined the sounds of country with rhythm and blues.

In the spring of 1963, and with a bit of money in his pocket to spend, George Harrison had acquired new equipment including hollow-bodied Gretsch Country Gentleman and Gretsch Tennessean guitars – popular at the time with the likes of Chet Atkins and others who went on to create the classic Nashville country sound. Harrison was hugely influenced by Atkins (listen to his solo for 'All My Loving' on With the Beatles) and all four, especially Ringo, were big fans of country-and-western music.

One of the few positives of constant US touring was that they were all strongly influenced by constant exposure to country radio stations while travelling up, down and across the American plains and, at that stage in their careers, learned a great deal from slicker, more experienced musicians. It was in 1964 in New York City that they also met with the new folk/country music superstar, Bob Dylan, for the first time – another major influence on Harrison who had encouraged his bandmates to listen to his early acoustic albums from 1962-64. It was an important meeting for all concerned: Dylan not only introduced them to cannabis but also to the concept of darker, more introspective musical themes, rather than what some might describe as 'happy-clappy pop songs'.

John Lennon's 'I'm a Loser' was undeniably not only influenced by, but also carbon-copied from the tone, style and structure of Dylan's typical

THE BEATLES ON VINYL

BEATLES '65

Released: 15 December 1964
Label: Capitol
UK: Not released
USA: No. 1

Side 1:
1. No Reply
2. I'm a Loser
3. Baby's in Black
4. Rock and Roll Music (Berry)
5. I'll Follow the Sun
6. Mr. Moonlight (Johnson)

Side 2:
1. Honey Don't (Perkins)
2. I'll Be Back
3. She's a Woman
4. I Feel Fine
5. Everybody's Trying to Be My Baby (Perkins)

Beatles '65 (although actually released late in 1964) includes eight of the 14 songs from Beatles For Sale (the first six in the same sequence) but adds 'I'll Be Back' – the last track from the UK *A Hard Day's Night* album, which was missing from the US version – plus both sides of the 'I Feel Fine'/'She's a Woman' UK single. (These two tracks are described on the rear cover notes as "enhanced" by Capitol's executive Dave Dexter Jr., converting the mono mixes into stereo.) Somewhat bizarrely, this US mash-up of two UK LPs and a single was described as the band's first "classic concept album" by *The Rolling Stone Record Guide.* Anyway, however described, it was hugely popular in the US and had sold almost 2 million copies by the end of 1964.

current output. The third track, 'Baby's in Black' continued the typical country-western theme covering dark storylines as a young man watches the girl he desires grieve for the death of another lover. Similarly 'I Don't Want to Spoil the Party' tells the gloomy tale of a boy who's been stood up at a party and, to avoid embarrassment, quietly sidles out furtively to look for her. Certainly these were not happy ditties in the style of 'She Loves You' just over a year before.

The opener, 'No Reply', was a great example of how much the band had developed and progressed over the last few months. Another rather sullen ballad, the song stood out as an outright narrative concerning romantic betrayal, which the band's music publisher Dick James (known for not holding back on criticism if he felt it necessary) recognised as such. Attending the recording session, he walked up to John Lennon and said, "You're getting better now. That was a complete story." Before that, according to Lennon, "...he thought my songs wandered off".

Noting the somewhat subdued tone of much of the album, producer George Martin commented: "They were rather war weary during *Beatles for Sale*. One must remember that they'd been battered like mad throughout 1964, and much of 1963. Success is a wonderful thing but it is very, very tiring."

Robert Freeman's excellent colour shot for the album's front cover clearly displayed the band's tiredness but, tired or not, they remained as enthusiastic as ever when it came to experimenting with recording equipment to achieve the unique sounds they were searching for. EMI had introduced a four-track desk in 1963 and the band now felt more confident to try out different techniques – encouraged by George Martin, who had already recognised their highly inventive approach. 'Eight Days a Week', for example, used fade-in for the introduction for the first time, while the single 'I Feel Fine' recorded at the same sessions similarly makes use of guitar feedback intentionally.

Released less than five months after *A Hard Day's Night* had hit the record stores in support of their first film, remaining at the top of the charts during that entire period, *Beatles for Sale* replaced it at No. 1 and stayed there for 11 weeks; its place in the Top 20 was held for 46 weeks. The public loved it and so did just about every music critic on the planet. Over the years, it seems to have lost some of its appeal to many, including George Martin, but he recognised that, "Artistically, they were poised to enter a new and potentially exciting chapter in their career together."

Bob Dylan agreed. Acknowledging the Beatles' huge influence on modern popular music, he later concluded: "They were doing things nobody was doing. Their chords were outrageous, just outrageous, and their harmonies made it all valid. You could only do that with other musicians. Everybody else thought they were for the teenyboppers, that they were gonna pass right away. But it was obvious to me that they had staying power. I knew they were pointing the direction of where music had to go."

Dylan's next album, *Bringing it All Back Home*, released in 1965, was his first to feature an electric band. The times, they were a-changing.

LEFT: *From left to right: Ringo, Paul, John, and George, circa 1965.*

HELP!

Released:	**6 August 1965**
Label:	**Parlophone**
Producer:	**George Martin**
Recorded:	**EMI Studios, London**
UK:	**No.1**
USA:	**Own version released**

STUDIO ALBUMS

Side 1:
1. Help!
2. The Night Before
3. You've Got to Hide Your Love Away
4. I Need You (Harrison)
5. Another Girl
6. You're Going to Lose That Girl
7. Ticket to Ride

Side 2:
1. Act Naturally (Russell-Morrison)
2. It's Only Love
3. You Like Me Too Much (Harrison)
4. Tell Me What You See
5. I've Just Seen a Face
6. Yesterday
7. Dizzy Miss Lizzy (Williams)

65

Help!, the band's fifth studio album, is often not afforded the level of respect and credit it deserves. It's certainly not their best album, but it's also far from being the worst.

While *Beatles for Sale* had been recognised as the band's country-and-western record, this was a much more folky, acoustic affair, with all three writers once again being strongly influenced by smoking huge amounts of dope and listening to Bob Dylan and his folk-rock followers such as the Byrds. Most apparent is John Lennon's 'You've Got to Hide Your Love Away' – a purely acoustic song that Lennon described as coming from "my Dylan period". At one point during the recording session, George Martin asked Lennon if he could try "not to sound too much like Dylan", so much was the influence seeping throughout the entire project. 'Tell Me What You See' was equally Dylan with a bit of the Byrds thrown in for good measure.

As always the Beatles had been under immense

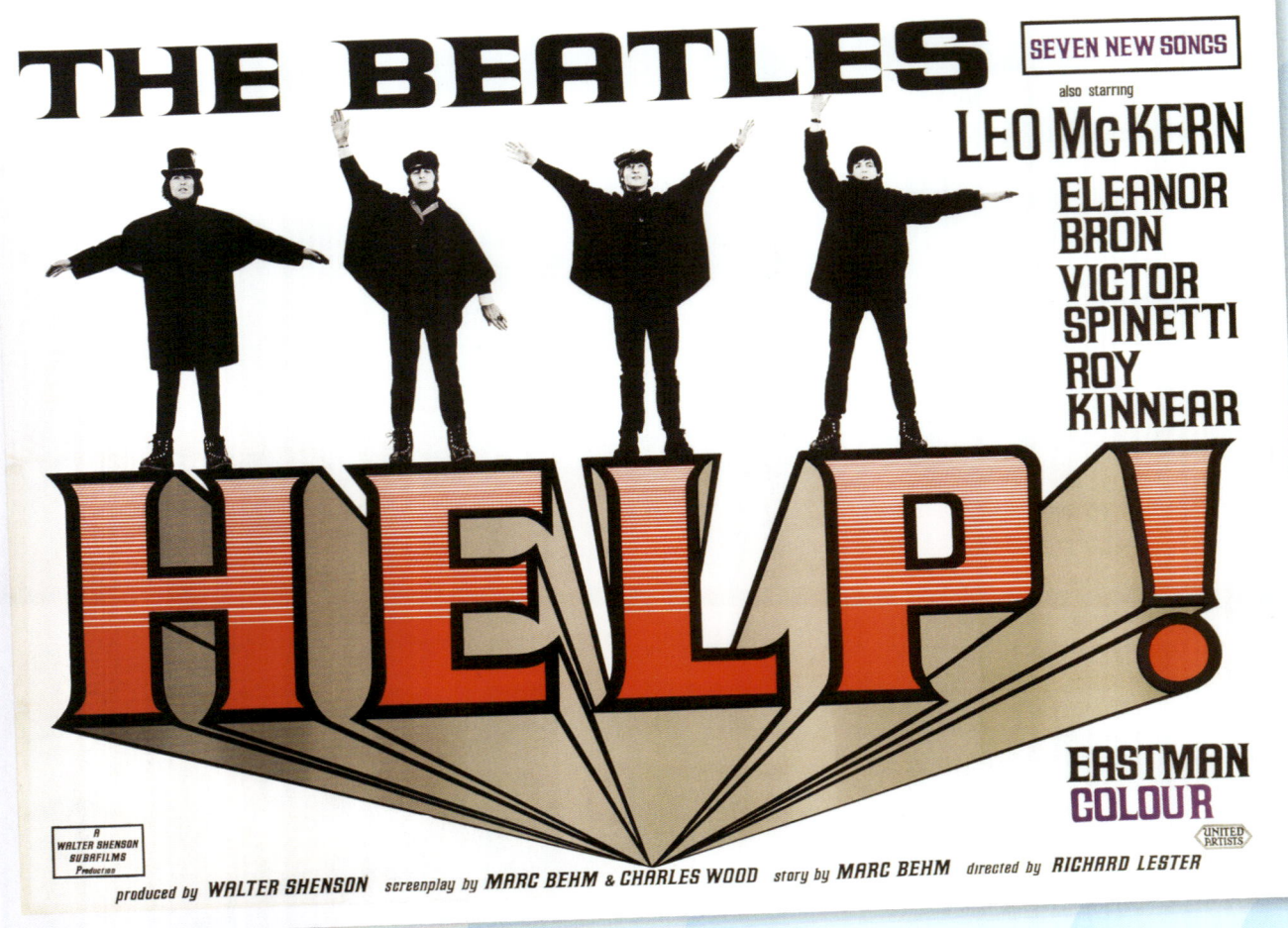

pressure to get the new album written and recorded with the slight inconvenience of having to take part in a big-budget, colour movie filmed across three countries (London and Salisbury Plain in the UK, the Austrian Alps and two Caribbean islands in the Bahamas). Despite such deadlines, McCartney's increased input and Harrison's boosted confidence had helped to make Lennon's life considerably easier, requiring just six new songs from him. Just two cover songs were added and would be the last until 'Maggie Mae' on *Let it Be* in 1970.

Not that Lennon was slacking: his six new numbers included two of the Beatles' best ever singles, 'Ticket to Ride' and the film title 'Help!', which had been handed over to John at short notice by director Dick Lester seven weeks into shooting, having decided that the film's working title of 'Eight Arms to Hold You' wasn't catchy enough. Within a few days Lennon had presented the song 'Help!' as a rather melancholy, mid-tempo number that, it transpired, portrayed his mental state of health and unhappiness at the time. George Martin's answer was just to speed things up as a way of getting the movie started; it was, after all, a spoof comedy.

STUDIO ALBUMS

The Beatles while filming Help!, Salzburg, Austria, 1965

Ringo's stunt double Mick Dillon with George Harrison on the set of the film Help! In the Bahamas, 1965

Stunt doubles (left) Joe Dunne (John Lennon) and Mick Dillon (Ringo Starr) on the set of the film Help! With Ringo In the Bahamas, 1965

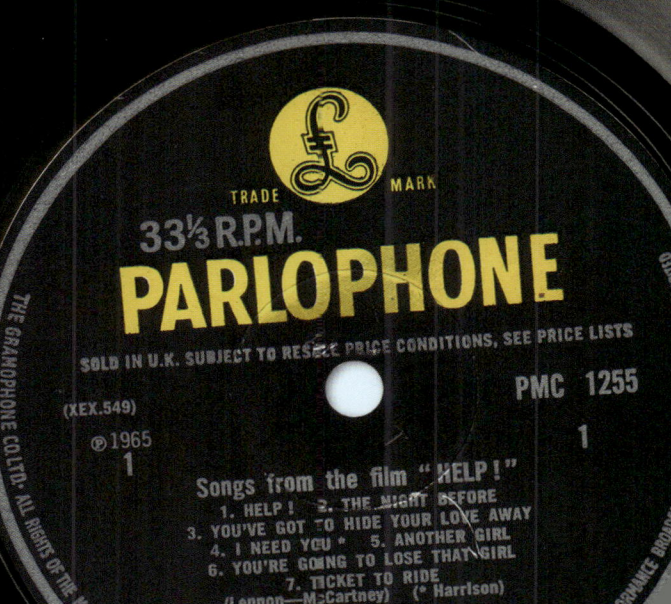

BEATLES VI

Released: 14 June 1965
Label: Capitol
UK: Not Released
USA: No. 1

Side 1:
1. Kansas City/Hey-Hey-Hey-Hey (Leiber-Stoller/Penniman)
2. Eight Days a Week
3. You Like Me Too Much (Harrison)
4. Bad Boy (Williams)
5. I Don't Want to Spoil the Party
6. Words of Love (Holly)

Side 2:
1. What You're Doing
2. Yes it Is
3. Dizzy Miss Lizzy (Williams)
4. Tell Me What You See
5. Every Little Thing

HELP!

Released: 13 August 1965
Label: Capitol
UK: Own Version Released
USA: No. 1

Side 1:
1. Help!
2. The Night Before
3. From Me to You Fantasy (instrumental arranged by Ken Thorne)
4. You've Got to Hide Your Love Away
5. I Need You (Harrison)
6. In the Tyrol (instrumental – Thorne)

Side 2:
1. Another Girl
2. Another Hard Day's Night (instrumental arranged by Ken Thorne)
3. Ticket to Ride
4. The Bitter End/You Can't Do That (Thorne/Lennon-McCartney – arranged by Ken Thorne)
5. You're Going to Lose That Girl
6. The Chase (instrumental arranged by Ken Thorne)

Once again the American version of *Help!* stuck to the more traditional format for a soundtrack, using songs from the film plus selections of the film's orchestral score, written and conducted (much to George Martin's chagrin) by Dick Lester's friend, the British film score composer, Ken Thorne. The US version is something of a collector's item because it includes a sitar-drenched, Bond-like 15-second intro before Lennon jumps in with the opening "Help!".

The seven non-film songs from Side 2 of the UK album were spread out through three American albums: three appeared on *Beatles VI* previously released two months earlier than the UK album and film premiere and largely made up of the six remaining tracks from *Beatles for Sale* plus two Larry Williams covers recorded specifically for the US market; two followed on *Rubber Soul* in December that year; and the follow-up album *Yesterday and Today* released in June 1966 made use of the remaining two songs. Despite half of the tracks being decimated, Capitol Records' version of *Help!* slowly climbed the charts and made it to No. 1 in the second week of September, remaining there for nine weeks.

McCartney's increased input to this album had only risen to four, but what a collection. Only 'The Night Before' and 'Another Girl' made it into the film soundtrack – both decent folk-tinged pop songs to lift the mood. On Side 2 is an even better track that should have been included, the superb love-at-first-sight folk song, 'I've Just Seen a Face' with its dramatic Spanish guitar intro played by Harrison. The other one that didn't make it onto the screen was one of his, or anybody else's, greatest ever compositions, 'Yesterday'. It wasn't used in the film because it just didn't fit. Anywhere else, it fitted perfectly.

As for George Harrison, 'I Need You' was his first song on a Beatles album since 'Don't Bother Me' on With the Beatles back in 1963; such a lack of input had badly affected his confidence as a songwriter. 'I Need You' (the better of his two offerings) being included in the soundtrack was a major boost for him.

It was also during the filming of Help!, at Twickenham Film Studios, that George, for the first time, saw a sitar being used in a scene set in an Indian restaurant. George was instantly fascinated by the sound and, after chatting to the Indian musicians taking part, bought himself a record by the Indian virtuoso, Ravi Shankar. Next step was to buy himself a sitar from a store in London. Within a short space of time, being a Beatle, he had arranged to meet Shankar and have some lessons with him. His compositional influences would never be quite the same again. Ringo, on the other hand, stuck to country music he loved and contributed a great rendition of 'Act Naturally' for the Help! LP.

The Beatles' intentions for the film was an off the wall mix of the Marx Brothers' Duck Soup combined with a sort of spoof James Bond espionage thriller, which kind of works as long as you don't analyse it too much. The humour elements are definitely influenced by the UK's surrealistic but hugely successful BBC radio programme, The Goon Show. Director Dick Lester had connections through previous film work with Peter Sellers, while George Martin had also produced records for The Goon Show and for Sellers, including Songs for Swingin' Sellers which all of the Beatles were big fans of.

The album cover shows the Beatles with their arms positioned in a way that is meant to spell out the word 'HELP' in semaphore – once again the idea of photographer Robert Freeman. In fact, visually, 'HELP' didn't look too good so Freeman repositioned their arms purely for artistic reasons. Whatever it means, it looks graphically superb, with the album title and band name just tucked away on the edges. The blue-clad Fab Four image against a plain white background says it all and no-one needed anything else to persuade them to buy this LP.

With the film premiere for Help! taking place in London on 29 July 1965, the album was released in the UK eight days later and went straight to No. 1, knocking The Sound of Music soundtrack into second place for nine weeks until Julie Andrews won it back in October. Help! was also nominated in 1966 for a Grammy in the 'Album of the Year' category – the first pop band to achieve such recognition.

RUBBER SOUL

Released:	**3 December 1965**
Label:	**Parlophone**
Producer:	**George Martin**
Recorded:	**EMI Studios, London**
UK:	**No.1**
USA:	**Own version released**

STUDIO ALBUMS

Side 1:
1. Drive My Car
2. Norwegian Wood (This Bird Has Flown)
3. You Won't See Me
4. Nowhere Man
5. Think for Yourself (Harrison)
6. The Word
7. Michelle

Side 2:
1. What Goes On (Lennon-McCartney-Starkey)
2. Girl
3. I'm Looking Through You
4. In My Life
5. Wait
6. If I Needed Someone (Harrison)
7. Run For Your Life

So we've arrived at *Rubber Soul*, the Beatles' transitional album, or "the pot album" as John Lennon preferred to describe it, thanks to its dope and LSD-induced brilliance. Either way, this was the album when the Beatles (although still influenced by the likes of Elvis, Bob Dylan, the Byrds and a wide variety of black soul singers) developed into something completely new.

There's an argument that *Rubber Soul* isn't drastically different to what had gone before just six months earlier on *Help!* – another Beatles transition album, but in truth, aren't they all? *Rubber Soul* offers an equal mix of pop, soul, folk-rock and country-and-western music, but while *Help!* took giant steps towards what lay ahead, *Rubber Soul* represented more of a giant leap for Beatle-kind. A "departure record", said Ringo. So what was so different?

During the course of four weeks recording in EMI Studios under the comforting wing of George Martin, for the first time in their career the band had no other commitments to worry about. No film, very little TV/radio work and no gigs. After a month on tour in the USA, including the infamous concert for over 55,000 screaming fans at the Shea Stadium in Hollywood, the band made the decision they'd had enough.

Despite the touring chaos, being in the States for a month had brought many positives – meeting up with Bob Dylan once again, and for the first and only time with their hero, Elvis Presley; listening to the latest soul music pouring out of Motown and Stax labels, at a time when stars such as Smokey Robinson and the Miracles, Diana Ross and the Supremes, the Temptations, the Four Tops, Marvin Gaye, James Brown, Wilson Pickett and Otis Redding were beginning to gain dominance in the US charts; and discovering there were so many creative alternatives in life that were preferable to being screamed at by fans and hassled eight days a week by the media: books, theatre, the arts, bohemian acquaintances and experimenting with hallucinogenic drugs, for example.

THE BEATLES ON VINYL

STUDIO ALBUMS

ABOVE: *Production line at E.M.I. factory in Hayes Middlesex where the new Beatles LP Rubber Soul is being manufactured 24th November 1965*

In the studio, for the first time, the Beatles were in charge. George Martin had released his four ugly ducklings to find their own way in the big world. *Rubber Soul* was one of his first projects after leaving EMI to co-found Associated Independent Recording (AIR) based in Oxford Street, London. He had given the Beatles the space and time they needed to expand and set their ambitions much higher. *Rubber Soul*, he said, was "the first album to present a new, growing Beatles to the world... For the first time we began to think of albums as art on their own, as complete entities."

George Harrison agreed, stating during an interview in the Nineties that *Rubber Soul* was his favourite Beatles album: "The most important thing about it was that we were suddenly hearing sounds we weren't able to hear before. Also, we were being more influenced by other people's music and everything was blossoming at that time – including us."

Before the recording sessions, McCartney was given a new, solid-body, Rickenbacker bass providing a much more aggressive, punchier sound than his boomy, hollow-body Hofner. The opening, soul-influenced 'Drive My Car' demonstrates this new bass tone perfectly, allowing McCartney to contribute far more melodic bass lines, such as 'You Won't See Me', or George Harrison's 'Think For Yourself', making use of a newly-acquired bass fuzz-box.

John Lennon and George Harrison both used new Fender Stratocasters for the first time during the *Rubber Soul* sessions – listen to Harrison's lead guitar on Lennon's psychedelia-inspired 'Nowhere Man' as a good example. *Rubber Soul* also saw his first use of the sitar on Lennon's 'Norwegian

THE BEATLES ON VINYL

MAIN IMAGE: George Harrison records on a Rickenbacker 12-string electric guitar in the studio, circa 1965

RUBBER SOUL

Released: 3 December 1965
Label: Capitol
UK: Own version released
USA: No. 1

Side 1:
1. I've Just Seen a Face
2. Norwegian Wood (This Bird Has Flown)
3. You Won't See Me
4. Think for Yourself (Harrison)
5. The Word
6. Michelle

Side 2:
1. It's Only Love
2. Girl
3. I'm Looking Through You
4. In My Life
5. Wait
6. Run For Your Life

The American *Rubber Soul* contained 10 of the original 14 songs and two tracks that had been withheld from *Help!* earlier in the year. Dropped were 'Drive My Car', 'Nowhere Man', 'What Goes On' and Harrison's 'If I Needed Someone', which would all appear on the US album *Yesterday and Today* the following year. Capitol dropped those four numbers and opened with McCartney's 'I've Just Seen a Face' from *Help!* in an effort to present more of an acoustic, folk-rock album. Strange decision, then, to remove 'Nowhere Man', which was certainly folkier than several of the songs that were retained. Surprising also that they didn't come up with a more folky or creative title: 'Beatles VIII', maybe?

STUDIO ALBUMS

Wood'. Throughout the album the band made use of a Hammond organ with it's swirling Leslie speaker cabinet along with a harmonium pump organ for the first time on the funky 'The Word' and the baroque-influenced single 'We Can Work it Out', recorded during *Rubber Soul*.

Ringo was playing various unusual percussive instruments during the sessions as well as a new Ludwig drum kit presented to him by the company in New York that year. He also takes lead vocals on the country-and-western number, 'What Goes On', the only Beatles song attributed to Lennon-McCartney and himself.

Side 2 continues with 'Girl' with its Greek bouzouki-sounding guitar parts; McCartney's folky 'I'm Looking Through You' concerning his troubled relationship with Jane Asher; Lennon's brilliant, Smokey Robinson-inspired 'In My Life' with its baroque piano solo played by George Martin; the Byrds-influenced 'If I Needed Someone' written by Harrison with its Indian drone background. Only 'Wait', written months earlier during the *Help!* sessions and the Elvis-inspired final song 'Run For Your Life' closely resemble the traditional Beatles sounds everyone had come to expect and felt comfortable with.

Not everyone took to the 'new sounds' immediately when they heard *Rubber Soul* for the first time. It took a while to sink in, but once etched into Beatles fans' grey matter, proved difficult to remove from the turntable. The album made it to No. 1 in the UK and USA and remained in the Top 10 until July the following year. It normally appears in the Top 100 albums of all time in just about any poll since the Sixties, and had an impact on the likes of psychedelia, pop-baroque, folk-rock and prog-rock – in fact, just about everything else that was to come. *Rubber Soul* is, in short, a genuine classic album – the first of five such remarkable achievements from the Beatles over the next four years. Within eight months would arrive *Revolver*.

"The most important thing about it was that we were suddenly hearing sounds we weren't able to hear before"

George Harrison MBE

REVOLVER

Released:	**5 August 1966**
Label:	**Parlophone**
Producer:	**George Martin**
Recorded:	**EMI Studios, London**
UK:	**No.1**
USA:	**Own version released**

STUDIO ALBUMS

Side 1:
1. **Taxman** (Harrison)
2. **Eleanor Rigby**
3. **I'm Only Sleeping**
4. **Love You To** (Harrison)
5. **Here, There and Everywhere**
6. **Yellow Submarine**
7. **She Said, She Said**

Side 2:
1. **Good Day Sunshine**
2. **And Your Bird Can Sing**
3. **For No One**
4. **Doctor Robert**
5. **I Want to Tell You** (Harrison)
6. **Got to Get You into My Life**
7. **Tomorrow Never Knows**

Remarkable that, within eight months of creating the classic *Rubber Soul*, the Beatles could come up with something that, most people will agree, is even better. As we've mentioned, George Harrison prefers *Rubber Soul*, regarding it and *Revolver* as volumes one and two of an album created using the same blueprint. It's a valid argument (how could it not be?), but if you listen to or even just view the two albums side by side (with German artist and musician Klaus Voormann's wonderful cover artwork), it's pretty clear that, with *Revolver*, the Beatles have made significant progress once again.

Harrison's 'Taxman' (partially inspired by the 'Batman' TV theme tune) opens the album, the first of his songs granted that accolade, and kicks things off well with its lyrical political digs, funky chords and a brilliant guitar solo surprisingly played by McCartney in addition to his inventive bass lines. It's Harrison's song but McCartney steals the show and follows on with nothing less than 'Eleanor Rigby' – one of his greatest compositions. No guitar, no bass, no drums, just three-part harmonies from McCartney, Lennon and Harrison and a string arrangement put together by George Martin inspired by Bernard Herrmann's tight, staccato strings for the infamous shower scene in Hitchcock's *Psycho*. Now add the lyrics, to which all four Beatles contributed, and the result is just over two minutes of sheer perfection.

Follow that. Lennon does, with 'I'm Only Sleeping' – another forward development with its use of varispeed equipment to speed up or slow down frequencies, plus a backwards guitar solo from Harrison that was actually transcribed in reverse by Martin and performed as such – not just played backwards on a machine. Three tracks in and you can already sense where things are heading – every song takes another giant stride towards something that had rarely, if ever, been achieved before.

'Love You To' is George Harrison's most impressive Indian raga-based song so far, given his limited

experience of the genre, but is primarily played by experienced Asian musicians. Next up is McCartney's composition he has described as the song he is most proud of, 'Here, There and Everywhere'; that surprises many, but it is a charming love song much in keeping with Brian Wilson and the Beach Boys' themes at that time.

Next comes 'Yellow Submarine', which regularly takes a bashing by various critics but is, after all, a song written by McCartney aimed at children, and what's wrong with that? Great fun with its use of hooters, bells and whistles and recorded sound effects, plus a great lyric brilliantly sung by Ringo. Once heard, never forgotten. Finishing off Side 1 is Lennon's 'She Said She Said' – another of his LSD-inspired novellas based on a drug-induced discussion with the actor Peter Fonda, who had told Lennon, "I know what it's like to be dead," following a near-death experience as a child when he accidently shot himself in the stomach.

Flip over to Side 2, deep breath, and straight into McCartney's 'Good Day Sunshine' followed by Lennon's 'And Your Bird Can Sing' – two up-tempo numbers to raise the spirits after the darker themes on much of Side 1. McCartney then returns with another of his sublime two-minute ballads, 'For No One', inspired once again by his relationship with Jane Asher. The highlight is the beautiful French horn solo played by the Philharmonia Orchestra's Alan Civil, who basically made it up as the recording went along.

It's back to more serious themes through to the end of *Revolver* with Lennon's 'Doctor Robert' – a satire based on a medical friend notorious for providing all sorts of drugs – followed by Harrison's third contribution, 'I Want to Tell You', with its constant discorcant piano, and McCartney's soulful 'Got To Get You Into My Life', which, he later revealed, was "actually an ode to pot".

The finale is 'Tomorrow Never Knows', Lennon's musical adaptation of Timothy Leary's book *The Psychedelic Experience: A Manual Based on The Tibetan Book of the Dead*, which compares the use of LSD with meditation in the search for spiritual enlightenment. With its reverse guitar and sitar, looped tape effects, varispeed vocals played through a revolving Leslie speaker, a repetitive drumbeat, Harrison's droned tambura, various instrument settings on a Mellotron and McCartney's laughter sped up to resemble a seagull, this was no three-minute pop song.

Overall, *Revolver* is an incredible piece of work. The Beatles had reached the destination to which the last two albums, *Help!* and *Rubber Soul*, had guided the band's collection of obsessed fans, musicians, musicologists and scholars towards over the last 12 months. None could have predicted this, but could anything improve on *Revolver*?

LEFT: *The Beatles, August 1966*

YESTERDAY AND TODAY

Released: 15 June 1966
Label: Capitol
UK: Not Released
USA: No. 1

Side 1:
1. Drive My Car
2. I'm Only Sleeping
3. Nowhere Man
4. Doctor Robert
5. Yesterday
6. Act Naturally (Russell-Morrison)

Side 2:
1. And Your Bird Can Sing
2. If I Needed Someone (Harrison)
3. We Can Work it Out
4. What Goes On (Lennon-McCartney-Starkey)
5. Day Tripper

REVOLVER

Released: 5 August 1966
Label: Capitol
UK: Own version released
USA: No. 1

Side 1:
1. Taxman (Harrison)
2. Eleanor Rigby
4. Love You To (Harrison)
5. Here, There and Everywhere
5. Yellow Submarine
6. She Said, She Said

Side 2:
1. Good Day Sunshine
2. For No One
3. I Want to Tell You (Harrison)
4. Got to Get You into My Life
5. Tomorrow Never Knows

Thankfully, *Revolver* was the final Beatles album to be given the Capitol Records track-listing mish-mash. Two months before its release, however, came *Yesterday and Today*, remembered primarily for its original 'butcher cover'. The photograph was taken in his London studio by Robert Whitaker, featuring the Fab Four dressed in blood-spattered white coats cuddling decapitated baby dolls and smeared with lumps of meat. Lovely. Why? There are various claims: A protest against Capitol butchering their albums? A protest against the USA's involvement in the Vietnam War? Or an artistic interpretation ridiculing the level of fan adulation the Beatles had had to tolerate? Whatever, many US record stores refused to stock the LP so the cover had to be quickly replaced with a rather tepid image (also taken by Whitaker at Brian Epstein's NEMS London offices) of the band sat in and around a packing trunk. Replacing the original image – often by gluing the new cover image over the top of the 'butcher cover' – cost Capitol a fortune.

The gory image had gone but the butchery remained as Capitol launched *Yesterday and Today* with two tracks from the UK album *Help!*, three from the not-yet released *Revolver* and four from *Rubber Soul*, plus both sides of the band's first double-A-sided single, 'We Can Work it Out'/'Day Tripper'. In effect, another compilation album, which neither Epstein or the band members were happy with.

The US version of *Revolver* was fairly straightforward compared to the chaos that had gone before: Just the three tracks that had appeared on Yesterday and Today two months earlier ('I'm Only Sleeping', 'And Your Bird Can Sing' and 'Doctor Robert') were dropped. Thankfully, no gore, and no more messing around with the Beatles' albums. Unless you include *Magical Mystery Tour*, but we'll forgive Capitol for that one.

SGT. PEPPER'S LONELY HEARTS CLUB BAND

Released:	**26 May 1967 (UK)**
	2 June 1967 (US)
Label:	**Parlophone**
Producer:	**George Martin**
Recorded:	**EMI Studios, London**
UK:	**No.1**
USA:	**No. 1**

Side 1:
1. Sgt. Pepper's Lonely Hearts Club Band
2. With a Little Help From My Friends
3. Lucy in the Sky with Diamonds
4. Getting Better
5. Fixing a Hole
6. She's Leaving Home
7. Being for the Benefit of Mr. Kite!

Side 2:
1. Within You Without You (Harrison)
2. When I'm Sixty-Four
3. Lovely Rita
4. Good Morning Good Morning
5. Sgt. Pepper's Lonely Hearts Club Band (Reprise)
6. A Day in the Life

Here we are, then. *Sgt. Pepper's Lonely Hearts Club Band*. The album against which all other albums before and since are measured. And we mean all – not just the Beatles' albums. For over 30 years it appeared at the top of virtually every critics' or fans' poll of 'The Greatest Albums of All Time'. But is it still? Has its long period of domination created an overall feeling of jaded disillusionment among Beatles fans and critics, relegating 'the world's greatest album' to a mid-table ranking? Or have renewed reassessments of *Revolver*, *The Beatles* and *Abbey Road* shifted the balance?

Whatever one feels about it now, there had certainly been nothing quite like *Sgt. Pepper* before it arrived. With its montages of extraordinary songs (and cover images) combined with studio experimentation and groundbreaking recording techniques (tape loops, backwards tape, tapes cut up and spliced randomly, speeding tapes up, slowing them down, using two tapes in sync...), *Sgt. Pepper* transported the Beatles and their fans to places they had never been to before.

Unsurprisingly, it was McCartney who had come up with the concept of the new album while returning from Kenya after holidaying with his girlfriend, Jane Asher, and the band's roadie, Mal Evans. On the flight home they'd been discussing the psychedelic music scene in California where bands with long-winded names (such as the 'West Coast Pop Art Experimental Band', and Janice Joplin's 'Big Brother and the Holding Company') were very much in vogue.

With his deep interest in the avant-garde and anything out of the ordinary, this was a vibe that appealed to McCartney: "I thought, let's not be ourselves. Let's develop alter egos... What would really be interesting would be to actually take on the personas of this different band. It would be a freeing element. I thought we can run this philosophy through the whole album: with this alter-ego band, it won't be us making all that sound, it won't be the Beatles, it'll be this other band..."

So, was it the world's first concept album? There are plenty of other contenders – Sinatra has several albums based on a theme back in the Fifties. What about John

Coltrane's *A Love Supreme* in 1965? Frank Zappa's *Freak Out*! (one of the first ever double-albums) was released almost a year earlier in June '66 and was regularly extolled by the Beatles. And the Beach Boys' *Pet Sounds* from May '66, had definitely enthused them, McCartney in particular. Brian Wilson, he said, had "… got some crazy stuff on there… We were inspired by it. And nicked a few ideas."

Back in Abbey Road, the band had discussed the idea of an album based on their Liverpool schooldays. Lennon had already offered 'Strawberry Fields Forever', to which McCartney had responded with 'Penny Lane', but it was George Martin who insisted these two great songs should be combined for another double-A-sided single and not appear on the LP. The "biggest mistake" of his professional career he confessed in later years. It begs yet another question: if he had included those two tracks on *Sgt. Pepper*, which others would have been dropped?

McCartney's concept of the album being performed by a fictional, Edwardian-era, military band won enough support from the other Beatles, at least initially, to get things underway. Sound engineer Geoff Emerick used recordings of an orchestra tuning up to open the album before the band kicked in with the rocky title song before segueing into 'With a Little Help From My Friends', sung by Ringo as the character Billy Shears.

It's a great opening five minutes, but the concept idea is pretty much dropped from that point onwards, apart from the title track reprise towards the end of Side 2. It was the Beatles' roadie and fixer, Neil Aspinall, who came up with the idea of the *Sgt. Pepper* character not only acting as a compere to open the show but also to close it. It works well, but just sticking a reprise towards the end of a record, a concept album does not make. As Lennon commented in *The Beatles Anthology*: "All my contributions to the album have absolutely nothing to do with the idea of *Sgt. Pepper* and his band, but it works, because we said it worked."

In reality, the songs that follow 'With a Little Help From My Friends' are connected only by a vague overall theme based on run-of-the-mill, rather mundane, everyday experiences; six of the remaining 10 songs are inspired simply (but brilliantly) by printed material, or the TV, or conversational phrases. Track 3 is Lennon's superb 'Lucy in the Sky with Diamonds', based on a painting by his young son Julian (which, he maintained to the end, had nothing to do with LSD) and lyrically by Spike Milligan's zany dialogue for *The Goon Show*.

'Getting Better' seems to be about a man working on improving his relationships with women; it was actually an expression regularly used by the Beatles' stand-in drummer Jimmie Nichol (who'd covered for Ringo when he was suffering with tonsillitis). Whenever asked how he was, he'd reply, "Getting better all the time," much to the band's amusement. 'Fixing a Hole' was another of McCartney's odes to pot and enjoying his own space in a new home, allowing his mind to wander. "It was the idea of me being on my own now," he said, "able to do what I want. If I want I'll paint the room in a colourful way." As above, nothing more, nothing less.

'She's Leaving Home' was written by McCartney after reading a newspaper article in the *Daily Mirror* concerning a young girl who'd gone missing, despite "having everything". Perfectly demonstrating McCartney's use of Sixties kitchen sink sentimentality similar to 'Eleanor Rigby', the Beatles play no instruments, only Paul and John singing a moving vocal duet; the string arrangement was put together by Mike

Leander (who went on to co-write many of Gary Glitter's hits) and features the harpist Sheila Bromberg – the first female instrumentalist to appear on a Beatles LP.

To finish Side 1, 'Being for the Benefit of Mr. Kite!' was inspired by a circus poster that Lennon bought in an antiques shop in Kent when filming a promo for 'Strawberry Fields Forever'/ 'Penny Lane'. The lyrics were virtually lifted from the poster, but John explained to George Martin that he wanted the backing track so accurate in representing circuses and fairgrounds that he could: "smell the sawdust". Martin understood, resulting in sound engineer, Geoff Emerick, throwing short lengths of tape of fairground music and steam organs up in the air before splicing them at random.

'Within You Without You' is the one track that some people aren't too keen on, with its melody and structure based on Indian classical music, but it is probably the best example of Harrison's commitment to Indian culture. Backed only by musicians from the Asian Music Circle in north London, the song was written initially on a harmonium at Klaus Voorman's house in London and, according to Jenny Boyd, George's sister-in-law at the time, is based on text from the book *Karma and Rebirth* written by an English barrister, Christmas Humphreys, in 1948.

'When I'm Sixty Four' was originally one of McCartney's early instrumental compositions written as a young teenager in admiration of musical comedy and vaudeville – the sort of music his dad, Jim, played regularly with his 'Jim Mac's Band'. It was when his father turned 64 in 1966 that Paul added new lyrics to the tune in recognition of his father's musical inspiration and encouragement.

'Lovely Rita' was also based on a newspaper article about a US meter maid combined with McCartney's brush with the law in the UK when served with a parking ticket by a female traffic warden. With its typical pub piano solo (played by George Martin), it again includes elements of whimsical music hall entertainment. Similarly, Lennon's 'Good Morning Good Morning' was inspired by a Kellogg's Corn Flakes TV advert he'd overheard one morning. It's a decent number with a brass score provided by three members of the British band, Sounds Incorporated, but Lennon wasn't too impressed himself, describing his own composition as "a piece of garbage".

Following the *Sgt. Pepper* reprise bringing the 'concept' to a conclusion, what follows is the album's most impressive and groundbreaking finale, 'A Day in the Life' – again based on *Daily Mail* newspaper stories concerning the Guinness heir Tara Browne (who the Beatles knew well) being killed in a car accident in London, and 4,000 potholes being reported in Blackburn, Lancashire, drawing attention to the poor condition of UK roads. Lennon wrote the opening two verses before McCartney's middle section portrays a man getting up for work but stressed because he's running late.

Verse three, referring to Dick Lester's film *How I Won the War*, which John had acted in, brings the song to a conclusion with its celebrated aural finale. Forty professional orchestral musicians were asked to play a scale from the lowest to the highest note on their instruments over a period of approximately 30 seconds, before culminating in an E-major chord played on various keyboards by the band and just about anyone else at hand. It all combines to create, as Lennon had requested, the sound of "the end of the world" – irrefutably the most dramatic climax in popular music.

THE BEATLES ON VINYL

To save money for EMI's still rather tight-fisted accountants, George Martin had taken seriously Ringo's light-hearted suggestion that they hire just half an orchestra and ask them to play it twice! Martin and Emerick doubled up the 40 musicians twice onto two, synched, 4-track recorders, resulting in the equivalent of 160 instruments to create an increasingly intense cacophony of sound that no-one had heard anything quite like before. As George Martin said: "There was a slight niggle of worry. I thought, 'Is the public ready for this?'"

Once completed and mixed, the Beatles took an acetate to their friend 'Mama' Cass Elliot's flat in Chelsea and played it at loud volume in the early hours of the morning with the windows wide open. The locals, it's claimed, realising what it was, dragged themselves out of bed and opened their windows to listen, and loved it. To many, this was more than just a new Beatles album; it was an event of worldwide cultural importance that was worth waking up for.

To balance things, not everyone was overly impressed, including two Fab Four members. Lennon stated a few years later that Sgt. Pepper wasn't his favourite LP because it was more Paul's album than the band's. Harrison wasn't too keen either: "It became an assembly process – just little parts and then overdubbing," he said. In the *New York Times*, critic Richard Goldstein described it as "an undistinguished collection of work". He continued: "The sound is a pastiche of dissonance and lushness. The mood is mellow, even nostalgic. But, like the cover, the overall effect is busy, hip and cluttered. Like an over-attended child, *Sgt. Pepper* is spoiled."

Yes, the album cover was cluttered, but few others would claim that Peter Blake's artistic concept (using Paul's sketches based on a photograph of Jim Mac's Band [his father's] musicians and friends gathered around its large bass drum) was anything other than brilliant. Photographed by Michael Cooper at his Chelsea studio with a giant backdrop of over 70, life-sized, inspirational characters largely chosen by the band, it was the icing on the cake. The artwork also included all of the lyrics on the back of a garishly psychedelic gatefold sleeve, plus additional cardboard cut-out inserts inside… it took the concept of an album to a whole new dimension. Fans around the world had been turned on; minds had been well and truly blown.

Straight to No. 1 almost immediately all around the world, *Sgt. Peppers Lonely Hearts Club Band* held that position for 27 weeks in the UK chart and 15 in the US Hot 100, and changed the way people listened to and appreciated popular music. The greatest album of all time? Not necessarily. But probably the most important.

Sgt. PEPPER'S LONELY HEARTS CLUB BAND
50th ANNIVERSARY LIMITED EDITION DOUBLE-LP

Expanded 180-gram 2LP vinyl package released in 2017 features a new stereo mix on the first LP produced by George Martin's son, Giles. The second disc has previously unreleased alternate takes for all 13 songs, newly mixed in stereo and sequenced in the same order as the original album.

STUDIO ALBUMS

MAGICAL MYSTERY TOUR

Released:	**27 November 1967 (US)**
	19 November 1976 (UK)
Label:	**Capitol and Parlophone**
Producer:	**George Martin**
Recorded:	**MI and Chappell Studios, London**
UK:	**No. 2 (as EP);**
	No. 31 (as US import LP);
	UK release did not chart
USA:	**No. 1**

STUDIO ALBUMS

Side 1:
1. Magical Mystery Tour
2. The Fool on the Hill
3. Flying (Lennon-McCartney-Harrison-Starkey)
4. Blue Jay Way (Harrison)
5. Your Mother Should Know
6. I Am the Walrus

Side 2:
1. Hello Goodbye
2. Strawberry Fields Forever
3. Penny Lane
4. Baby You're a Rich Man
5. All You Need is Love

67

As if the masterpiece *Sgt. Pepper's Lonely Hearts Club Band* wasn't sufficient for one year's output from the world's greatest rock band, they produced yet another impressive album (that wasn't really an album) just six months later.

Following the death of manager Brian Epstein in August 1967 as the result of an accidental overdose of barbiturates, Paul persuaded his bandmates that they should continue with their latest project, the first under the auspices of the Beatles' newly formed business conglomerate, Apple Corps. *Magical Mystery Tour* was, once again, largely Paul's idea, loosely based on the US author Ken Kesey's 'Merry Pranksters' – a group of hippy writers, artists and friends who travelled across the US in a multi-coloured school bus.

Without any guidance or organisational input now possible from Brian Epstein, the self-made, 52-minute, TV movie crawled rather too mysteriously around the UK's West Country and

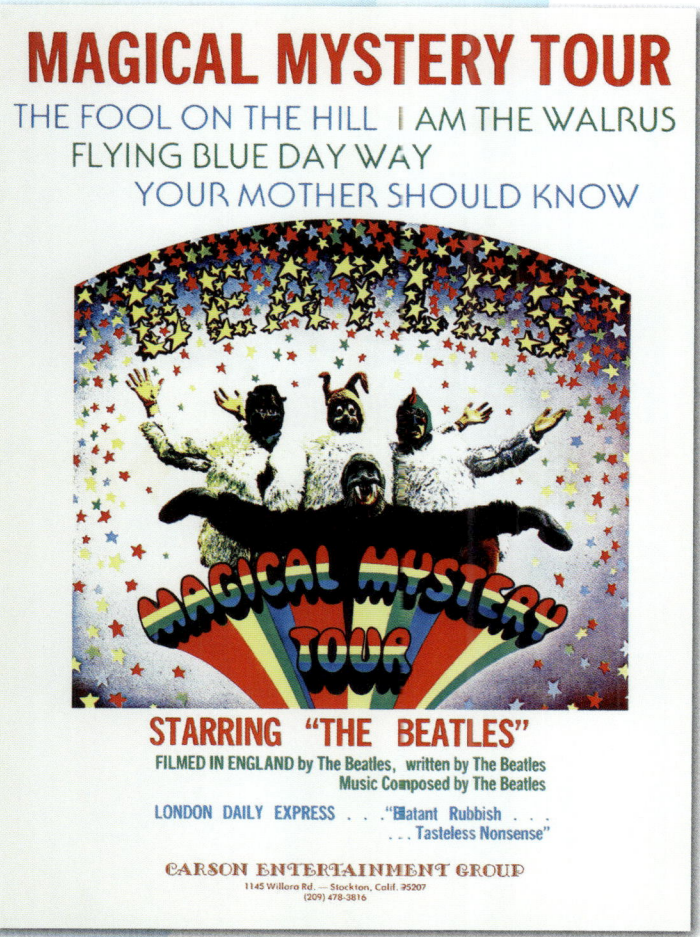

Kent and ultimately proved to be something of a disaster. Broadcast by the BBC on Boxing Day 1967, the British media loved an opportunity to knock the band off their cultural pedestal and tore the film to shreds – the Beatles' first major disappointment.

While many people now consider the *Magical Mystery Tour* LP to be part of the Beatles' catalogue, it was originally released as an album only in the US; in the UK it was a beautifully packaged, gatefold, six-song double-EP that made it to No. 2 in the charts – prevented from becoming the first EP to make it to the top of the singles charts only by the Beatles' own No. 1 single 'Hello, Goodbye'.

Although the film had some amusing, Monty Python-esque moments, overall the soundtrack was much better than the movie itself, featuring some of McCartney's best songs since *Sgt. Pepper*. Side 1 was made up of those six original numbers, starting with the film's energetic title track, followed by his superb 'The Fool on the Hill'; it had been written during the *Sgt. Pepper* sessions and could easily have been included were it not for McCartney's even better ballad ' She's Leaving Home'.

Side 1 takes a slight dip in the middle with the Mellotron-soaked, jazzy-blues instrumental 'Flying' (the first song credited to all four Beatles) and Harrison's once again Indian-inspired 'Blue Jay Way'. McCartney then returns with 'Your Mother Should Know', a sort of pub-singalong in the style of his father's piano playing days back in the Forties and Fifties. From one extreme to the other, the film soundtrack ends with Lennon's wonderful 'I Am the Walrus'.

For the US album, Side 2 comprised of five more tracks: both sides of the Beatles' first two 1967 singles plus the official A-side, 'Hello Goodbye', of what should have been a double-A-sided single with 'I Am the Walrus.' Despite disappointment at the way the LP's track listing had been put together by Capitol without the band's approval, for once a US mash-up worked pretty well. The result was a top-selling, feel-good, psychedelic-themed album that glued together well and has become increasingly popular over the last 50-odd years on both sides of the Atlantic.

Although it had not been too difficult in Great Britain to buy a copy of *Magical Mystery Tour* as a US import, it was not until November 1976 that, as part of a big sales push by EMI once their contract with the band expired, the album was finally released as an LP in the UK. Releasing it without any great support, however, proved to be a mistake. It was six years since the Beatles had split and the UK music scene had changed considerably; the *Magical Mystery Tour* took another wrong turn and did not find its way into the UK charts.

MAIN IMAGE: *John Lennon filming the television musical film 'Magical Mystery Tour' in a field near Newquay, Cornwall on 14th September 1967*

STUDIO ALBUMS

THE BEATLES ON VINYL

THE BEATLES
(aka the 'White Album')

Released:	**22 November 1968**
Label:	**Apple**
Producer:	**George Martin**
Recorded:	**EMI and Trident Studios, London**
UK:	**No. 1**
USA:	**No. 1**

STUDIO ALBUMS

Side 1:
1. Back in the U.S.S.R.
2. Dear Prudence
3. Glass Onion
4. Ob-La-Di, Ob-La-Da
5. Wild Honey Pie
6. The Continuing Story of Bungalow Bill
7. While My Guitar Gently Weeps (Harrison)
8. Happiness is a Warm Gun

Side 2:
1. Martha My Dear
2. I'm So Tired
3. Blackbird
4. Piggies (Harrison)
5. Rocky Racoon
6. Don't Pass Me By (Starkey)
7. Why Don't We Do It in the Road?
8. I Will
9. Julia

Side 3:
1. Birthday
2. Yer Blues
3. Mother Nature's Son
4. Everybody's Got Something to Hide Except Me and My Monkey
5. Sexy Sadie
6. Helter Skelter
7. Long, Long, Long (Harrison)

Side 4:
1. Revolution 1
2. Honey Pie
3. Savoy Truffle (Harrison)
4. Cry Baby Cry
5. Revolution 9
6. Good Night

68

The Beatles, or the 'White Album', as it is better known, was very much the antithesis of *Sgt. Pepper's Lonely Hearts Club Band* when it arrived 18 months later. Most obvious was its plain white cover and barely legible embossed title in contrast to the Day-Glo, psychedelic colour-fest of its two predecessors, *Sgt. Pepper* and *Magical Mystery Tour*. Once on the record player it was also clear from the outset that the songs, production values and the level of studio trickery had also been dramatically downscaled. *The Beatles* wasn't an attempt to improve on *Sgt. Pepper* but to offer something completely different – exactly what the Rolling Stones would do with *Sticky Fingers* and *Exile on Main St* in 1971/72 and Fleetwood Mac with *Rumours* and *Tusk* in 1977/79 but, as ever, the Beatles did it first. In 1968, probably nobody else would have got away with it.

Most of the songs on the album were written during

their eight-week period from February to April at a Transcendental Meditation course in Rishikesh, India, with the Maharishi Mahesh Yogi. They'd previously met him at a seminar in Bangor, Wales, but had left early only when receiving the news that their manager Brian Epstein had died. So impressed had they been by the Maharishi that they'd decided to commit more seriously to his spiritual teachings.

Although the main intention of travelling to India was to meditate and attend the Maharishi's lectures, the band also wanted to escape the turmoil of being a Beatle. It was also the perfect opportunity for them to work on new songs for their forthcoming, as yet untitled, ninth album, and did they ever. Despite the only western instruments available during their stay being acoustic guitars, Lennon, McCartney and Harrison worked on and demoed well over 30 numbers, of which 17 would eventually appear on the 'White Album'. For the very first time, even Ringo wrote one by himself – a simple but effective country blues number 'Don't Pass Me By'

with its nice bluegrass fiddle part.

Also attending the course were Mike Love of the Beach Boys, the actress Mia Farrow and the Scottish folk singer Donovan, who helped Lennon learn how to fingerpick an acoustic guitar rather than just strum. Once mastered, John used the technique to write 'Dear Prudence' (about Mia Farrow's sister who was spending more time meditating than anyone else) and 'Julia' (his late mother).

None of the band members made it to the end of the course – Ringo and his wife Maureen were the first to leave after two weeks because he hated the food and Maureen struggled with the various flies and insects buzzing all around. McCartney and Jane Asher departed in mid-March as they both had other work commitments, while Harrison and Lennon remained almost until the course finished in April. Lennon left Rishikesh because he was missing Yoko and also uncomfortable after hearing rumours that the Maharishi had behaved inappropriately towards some of the women on the course. Lennon wrote a song for the new album ('Sexy Sadie') for that reason, although there was no evidence any such impropriety had actually taken place. 'Everybody's Got Something to Hide Except Me and My Monkey' was also written by Lennon based on an expression the Maharishi often used.

Lennon's wife Cynthia also attended the meditation course but it was there that John decided their

THE BEATLES ('WHITE ALBUM') 50th ANNIVERSARY DELUXE LIMITED EDITION DOUBLE-DOUBLE-LP

Expanded 180-gram 4LP vinyl package released in 2018 features a new stereo mix double-album taken from the original 4-track and 8-track session tapes and produced by George Martin's son, Giles, assisted by senior engineer, Sam Okell, and a team of audio engineers and restoration specialists at Abbey Road. The other double-LP includes what have become known as the 'Esher Demos', 27 songs recorded on acoustic guitars at George Harrison's house in Esher, Surrey, in May 1968.

loveless marriage must come to an end; once back in London, he left his wife and moved in with Yoko Ono. The two became not only devoted to one another but also regular heroin users; once recording got underway, Yoko sat in at almost every session. Straight away the feeling at Abbey Road Studios rapidly deteriorated; in a cold, fragmented atmosphere, arguments between the band, their partners, the studio technicians, simmered.

Even mild-mannered producer George Martin decided half way through the sessions that he needed a holiday and disappeared for almost a month, leaving his young protégé Chris Thomas (who went on to produce breakthrough albums for the likes of the Sex Pistols, Roxy Music and INXS,) in charge of production. Martin had found it very difficult to witness the Beatles' prolonged and painful break-up. "I felt emasculated by what was going on," he said. "I felt that I didn't have a role to play. I wasn't just going to walk out, having gone that far. But it was a tough time, really tough. They were so much at each other's throats."

More surprising still was softly-spoken sound engineer Geoff Emerick's decision to stop working with the Beatles altogether. Lennon had been guilty of bullying Emerick several times over the years and, on this occasion, had shouted at him acrimoniously and unfairly about the way he was recording John's guitar on 'Revolution 1'. Sensitive and deeply upset, Emerick worked under an increasingly dark cloud at Abbey Road for the next few weeks and was struggling with the album's rough edges compared to *Sgt. Pepper*.

When an unpleasant argument took place in July '68 between McCartney and George Martin while recording 'Ob-La-Di, Ob-La-Da', it pushed Emerick over the edge. The following day, he requested a transfer to other roles at EMI and didn't work with the Beatles again for over nine months. His place was taken by Ken Scott, who had already worked on various Beatles sessions over the previous year and would go on to work on major albums for David Bowie, Elton John and many others.

Truth was, nobody was having much fun and *The Beatles* ceased to be a band project; several songs were recorded solo, or with one or two of the other band members. Only 16 of the album's 30 tracks feature all four Beatles working together. At times the three main songwriters would be recording in three different studios, with Ringo flitting between them or, at times, sitting bored to tears in the studio's reception. No surprise that early in the sessions he also decided he'd had enough and left the band. It was almost three weeks before his bandmates persuaded him to come back and they were left with responsibility for playing drums on the two opening numbers – McCartney's 'Back in the U.S.S.R.' (a parody of Chuck Berry's 'Back in the U.S.A.') and Lennon's 'Dear Prudence' (the first Beatles song to be recorded on an eight-track machine). 'Glass Onion' was the first backing track recorded by the full band after Ringo's return.

'Ob-La-Di, Ob-La-Da' was written by McCartney as a light pastiche of reggae music and, although not popular with the other Beatles, went on to be a No. 1 hit later that year for the Scottish band, Marmalade. McCartney's brief 'Wild Honey Pie' links into Lennon's 'The Continuing Story of Bungalow Bill' which he wrote in response to an American visitor to Rishikesh who replaced meditation with hunting and shooting tigers. 'While My Guitar Gently Weeps' was the first of Harrison's four numbers, featuring a blistering guitar solo taken care of by his friend, Eric Clapton. Bringing Side 1 to an end is Lennon's 'Happiness Is a Warm Gun',

THE BEATLES ON VINYL

brilliantly constructed from several song fragments, hence the disjointed tempo and lyrical themes throughout that challenges any normal song structure.

Few would disagree that Side 1 is pretty damn good, continuing on Side 2 with McCartney's 'Martha My Dear' named after his sheepdog – another solo performance backed by orchestral musicians. It's followed by Lennon's 'I'm So Tired' written in India when he was having problems sleeping; 'Blackbird' is one of McCartney's most loved acoustic solo numbers, criticising civil rights issues in America; Harrison follows that with 'Piggies', his satire on the greediness of modern society. 'Rocky Raccoon' – another example of McCartney's music hall comedy – was the result of him jamming in India with Lennon and Donovan, followed by Ringo's first solo composition for the band.

McCartney's 'Why Don't We Do It in the Road?' – written in India after seeing two monkeys having sex in the street – is the first track that many would find disappointing despite its length of less than two

STUDIO ALBUMS

minutes, but he redeems himself with his beautiful ballad 'I Will' with its vocal bass line. Completing Side 2 is Lennon's equally lovely 'Julia' – the last song to be recorded for *The Beatles* and the only Beatles song Lennon performs by himself.

There's little point in progressing through the remaining 13 tracks on Sides 3 and 4 as, despite some highlights – McCartney's 'Mother Nature's Son' with George Martin's brass arrangement, Harrison's Dylan-inspired 'Long, Long, Long', and Lennon's anarchic 'Revolution 1' – it's the dreaded audio collage 'Revolution 9' (put together by Lennon, Harrison and Yoko in respect of the controversial German composer, Karlheinz Stockhausen) that's always been the main talking point. It is bonkers and, needless to say, McCartney wasn't too happy about its conclusion (we won't mention 'Wild Honey Pie' in response), but there will be people out there who genuinely regard it as the best track on the album. If you've never heard it, or at least never made it all the way through, give it another go; bizarrely it's the nearest thing on *The Beatles* to the wackier moments on *Sgt. Pepper*.

Fans and critics regularly refer to the sheer range, depth and diversity the Beatles managed to fit into their careers together over a 10-year period; *The Beatles* album manages to cram in maybe even more variety into four sides of what's regarded by many as the greatest double-album of all time. Yes, it's not all brilliant, or even good, but much of it is stunning: the work of three brilliant songwriters at the acme of their careers supported by a terrific drummer who manages to stay Ringo, stay sane and stay in time.

Play all four sides in the correct order and without skipping 'Revolution 9' and you're committing to a 90-minute, fun all the way, roller coaster ride through a thrilling collection of songs; there may be one or two places where you'll feel baffled, bemused or maybe even edgy, but that's the whole point. Some feel that a diversion to avoid some of the bumpy sections might have been a better option. Others consider it perfect just the way it is. It's only 53 years old so give it a bit more time before coming to any final conclusion.

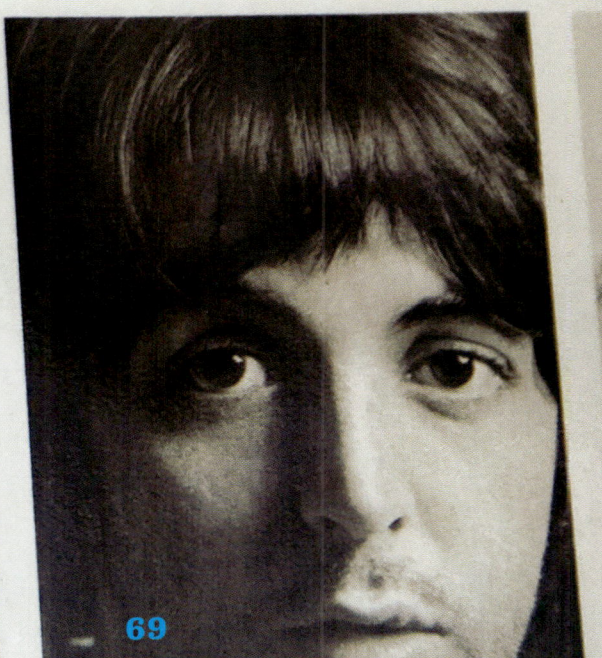

YELLOW SUBMARINE

Released:	**3 January 1969 (USA)**
	17 January 1969 (UK)
Label:	**Apple**
Producer:	**George Martin**
Recorded:	**EMI / De Lane Lea Studios, London**
UK:	**No. 3**
USA:	**No. 2**

Side 1:
1. Yellow Submarine
2. Only a Northern Song (Harrison)
3. All Together Now
4. Hey Bulldog
5. It's All Too Much (Harrison)
6. All You Need is Love

Side 2:
1. Pepperland (Martin)
2. Seat of Time (Martin)
3. Sea of Holes (Martin)
4. Sea of Monsters (Martin)
5. March of the Meanies (Martin)
6. Pepperland Laid Waste (Martin)
7. Yellow Submarine in Pepperland
(Lennon-McCartney, arranged by Martin)

Generally regarded as something of a backward step with only four 'new' numbers (and not particularly good ones) to fill Side 1, along with a title song that first appeared on *Revolver*, and the single 'All You Need is Love'. It comes nowhere near the high standard of work the Beatles had become known for and were now expected to produce every few months, which was totally unrealistic. The result was an album that will probably not be the one that hogs your turntable.

The project was basically a contractual obligation for the Beatles with the responsibility of supplying four new songs for an animated movie. Two of the songs ('All Together Now' and 'Hey Bulldog') were written and recorded specifically for the soundtrack, while George Harrison's 'Only a Northern Song' had been recorded during the *Sgt. Pepper* sessions but regarded (quite rightly) as a reject. His 'It's All Too Much' met a similar fate during the *Magical Mystery Tour* recordings although, with its LSD-induced guitar/keyboard droning, improvised trumpets and repetitive vocal references to David Bowie's 'Sorrow', would have fitted in very well.

Yellow Submarine was recorded before the 'White Album' and released two months later. An EP featuring the four new songs was also put together, but never released, which is understandable. If you're not a completist and don't have or don't want to buy *Yellow Submarine*, you can find those four tracks on *Mono Masters Volume 2*. A better option is probably to buy the film DVD and enjoy the songs (and George Martin's commendable orchestration work on Side 2) to appreciate the overall package. Especially if you're under 10 years old.

ABBEY ROAD

Released:	**26 September 1969**
Label:	**Apple**
Producer:	**George Martin**
Recorded:	**EMI, Olympic & Trident Studios , London**
UK:	**No. 1**
USA:	**No. 1**

STUDIO ALBUMS

Side 1:
1. Come Together
2. **Something** (Harrison)
3. Maxwell's Silver Hammer
4. Oh! Darling
5. **Octopus's Garden** (Starkey)
6. I Want You (She's So Heavy)

Side 2:
1. **Here Comes the Sun** (Harrison)
2. Because
3. You Never Give Me Your Money
4. Sun King
5. Mean Mr. Mustard
6. Polythene Pam
7. She Came In Through the Bathroom Window
8. Golden Slumbers
9. Carry That Weight
10. The End
11. Her Majesty

It may have been the final album recorded by the Beatles together but *Abbey Road* is full of great songs and an element of happiness that had long been missing within the band, both through the recording of the fractured 'White Album' and the miserable process of filming and recording *Let It Be*.

George Martin was the last person to expect to hear anything from the Beatles as their career neared the end. Although saddened by what had happened, he felt it a release to no longer be under the pressure of producing Beatles LPs and was looking forward to working with other artists. He was very surprised to receive a call from Paul McCartney asking him to come back to Abbey Road Studios to produce their next album. "Only if you let me produce it the way we used to," he replied. "We do want to do that," said Paul, meaning all of them, including John, who had previously complained about George's "production shit" before, ironically, handing over the *Let it Be* tapes to Phil Spector.

Things got underway very well when John and Paul went into Abbey Road with George Martin and, for the first time in nine months, sound engineer Geoff Emerick (now working for Apple Corps), to record the single 'The Ballad of John and Yoko'. With neither Ringo or George Harrison available and John wanting to get the single released as quickly as possible, it was down to himself and McCartney to work together for a whole day. It didn't bode well, given the anguish of the last few months but, surprisingly, they seemed to enjoy themselves. As Geoff Emerick described it in his autobiography, *Here, There and Everywhere*, "they reverted to being two old school chums, all the nastiness of recent months swept under the rug and replaced by the sheer joy of making music together."

Even better was the way this newfound, Lennon-McCartney brotherliness was contagious as all four band members got together to record Harrison's 'Something' two days later – a return to normality without any trace of disarray, tedium, frustration or anger. Even harder to believe was McCartney describing 'Something' as the best song Harrison had ever written and Lennon saying it was his favourite song on the album. Ringo agreed: "It was beautiful. George was blossoming as a songwriter." Spooky. Were they all on drugs or something?

Before 'Something', 'Come Together' was the opening song, loosely based on Chuck Berry's 'You Can't Catch Me'. A great song made up of more Lennon gobbledegook lyrics but with the mistake of leaving in the opening line "Here come old flat top" being lifted from Berry's lyrics, which had to be settled in court. Ironically, Harrison's first line for 'Something' ("Something in the way she moves") was lifted from James Taylor's first line and title of the opening song on his debut album; as he'd just signed to Apple Records, however, it was unlikely he'd be telling George Harrison he'd see him in court as well.

McCartney's first song on the album, 'Maxwell's Silver Hammer', had been written for the 'White Album' but rejected by his bandmates as "too complicated". Studio tension returned as Paul insisted on the track being included on the new album, requiring endless takes; John hated the song, described it as "more of Paul's granny music", and left the session.

Lennon did have a valid excuse in as much as he and his family had been involved in a car accident while on holiday in Scotland and been hospitalised for six days with serious cuts and bruises. Worst of all was that doctors had told Yoko, who was pregnant at the time, that she needed lots of bed rest; most would stay at home, but John's answer was to order a bed from Harrods and have it delivered to Abbey Road. Above the bed he attached a microphone so that Yoko could communicate with the band whenever she felt it necessary. Dark clouds appeared in Studio 2 and darkened, but luckily blew over.

'Oh! Darling' was also written by McCartney as a Fifties-style parody; to get an authentic Fifties vibe, he attempted the vocals over several days because he "wanted it to sound as though I'd been performing it on stage all week". 'Octopus's Garden' was the second of Ringo's enjoyable (if rather similar) solo compositions. Written during a holiday in Sardinia with his family aboard Peter Sellers's yacht, the song was inspired by an octopus served for lunch when they were expecting fish and chips.

'I Want You (She's So Heavy)' was written by Lennon about his relationship with Yoko and originally recorded in February 1969 at Trident Studios in London. A second version was produced in April at Abbey Road and the two versions were combined but not completed until August, making this the last track ever to be worked on by all four Beatles. Even longer than 'Hey Jude', the song's dramatic, 5-minute, jazzy climax features Billy Preston on keyboards and George Harrison's recently purchased Moog synthesizer to create a whooshing, white noise sound that, after 7 minutes and 44 seconds, Emerick is told by Lennon to "cut it right there". Thus, *Abbey Road's* Side 1 (and the Beatles' career) ends in startling silence.

As if Harrison needed to demonstrate his development as a songwriter, 'Here Comes the Sun' opens Side 2, having been written in Eric Clapton's garden in Surrey during a break from stressful Beatles meetings at the Apple Corps offices. Lennon was still recuperating from his car accident and did not perform on the track, but George's new toy, the Moog synthesizer, makes another appearance during the brilliant chorus.

Lennon's 'Because' was inspired by listening to Yoko playing Beethoven's 'Moonlight Sonata' on the piano. He asked her to play the chords in reverse and based the song on that sequence. With its complex three-part harmonies, it's probably the most difficult vocal challenge the Beatles ever recorded, with Harrison's Moog synthesizer appearing once again alongside George Martin's opening on harpsichord.

Now begins the stunning, 16-minute medley of at least eight (or more, depending on how you look at it) short songs, written over several months during the 'White Album' and 'Get Back' sessions. Harmoniously combined by McCartney and Martin into something rather wonderful, there are Beatles fans out there who consider the result to

be something created mystically by deeper forces. McCartney's explanation is more candid: "We had decided to gather up our fragments of songs we hadn't quite finished and create a train of thoughts that could bring the album to a close." Genius, or a way of digging themselves out of a hole. Either way, it's masterful.

'You Never Give Me Your Money' (aimed at Beatles manager, Allen Klein) opens the medley, in itself based on several McCartney fragments, and featuring some of his best vocals and bass playing ever. Lennon's 'Sun King', which, like 'Because', highlights their triple-tracked harmonies. Two more short, one-minute, Lennon numbers – 'Mean Mr. Mustard' (written in India) and 'Polythene Pam' (with its broad scouse, nasal vocal) blend perfectly into four more McCartney songs, 'She Came In Through the Bathroom Window' (written after a fan broke into his house and stole a picture of his father), 'Golden Slumbers' (based on a 17th-century poem 'Cradle Song' for which he composed new music), 'Carry That Weight' (repeating elements of 'You Never Give Me Your Money'), and closing with

STUDIO ALBUMS

'The End' featuring Ringo's only ever recorded drum solo and three two-bar lead guitar solos played by McCartney, Harrison, and Lennon, repeated twice. Guitars stop, staccato piano chords begin, three-part harmony vocals, a Shakespearian-like piece of poetry, guitar fills before orchestral strings and brass bring it all to an end. A tear-jerker. Perfect for funerals. The end. Or is it?

Twenty seconds later, almost as always, McCartney has the last word with the brief, but wonderful, 'Her Majesty'. It was meant to form part of the medley between 'Mean Mr. Mustard' and 'Polythene Pam' but didn't quite fit. Twenty-three seconds of a song fragment wasn't worth worrying about so Paul told the engineer, John Kurlander, to dump it. Luckily for all, he didn't, because George Martin had taught his engineers never to dump anything. He left it on the tape as a rough mix but didn't quite cut it precisely; the final, crashing chord of 'Mean Mr. Mustard' wakes us all up after 20 seconds of silence. It wasn't meant to be like that, but the Beatles loved it, and left it in.

From the hundreds, thousands of reviews and comments made about the Beatles' *Abbey Road*, John Mendelsohn in *Rolling Stone* magazine summed it up most adroitly: "That the Beatles can unify seemingly countless musical fragments and lyrical doodlings into a uniformly wonderful suite, as they've done on Side 2, seems potent testimony that no, they've far from lost it, and no, they haven't stopped trying... they've achieved here the closest thing yet to Beatles freeform, fusing more diverse intriguing musical and lyrical ideas into a piece that amounts to far more than the sum of those ideas."

George Martin deserves the final say: It was "like the old days. They wanted me to exert control the way I did in the *Pepper* days. So I did, and *Abbey Road* proved to be a very happy album. They'd been disliking each other and having punch-ups, but now they came together and collaborated very well. I was very pleased that the group went out on a note of harmony and not one of discord."

And in the end...

ABBEY ROAD
50th ANNIVERSARY
DELUXE LIMITED EDITION
TRIPLE LP

Expanded 180-gram 3LP vinyl package released in 2019 features a new stereo mix of the album taken from the original 8-track session tapes and produced by George Martin's son, Giles, assisted by Abbey Road's senior engineer, Sam Okell. The other two LPs include 40 tracks taken from studio recordings during the *Abbey Road* sessions. Includes a four-page insert in a lift-top box.

LET IT BE

Released:	**8 May 1970 (UK)**
	18 May (USA)
Label:	**Apple & Capitol**
Producer:	**Phil Spector**
Recorded:	**Apple Corps roof and Apple, EMI and Twickenham Film Studios, London**
UK:	**No. 1**
USA:	**No. 1**

STUDIO ALBUMS

Side 1:
1. Two of Us
2. Dig a Pony
3. Across the Universe
4. I Me Mine (Harrison)
5. Dig It (Lennon-McCartney-Harrison)
6. Let it Be
7. Maggie Mae (traditional arranged by Lennon-McCartney-Harrison-Starkey)

Side 2:
1. I've Got a Feeling
2. One After 909
3. The Long and Winding Road
4. For You Blue (Harrison)
5. Get Back

In January 1969, three months after finishing the 'White Album', rehearsals had got underway at Twickenham Film Studios as part of Paul McCartney's concept for a TV documentary about the Beatles' preparation to return to performing live in a series of concerts at the Roundhouse venue in north London. It was also an attempt to rekindle their enthusiasm for playing as a good, old-fashioned, rock 'n' roll band, just as they'd been back in 1960 when their adventure began. In reality, it proved to be little more than McCartney's pipedream.

The filmed rehearsals, originally known as the 'Get Back' sessions, took place in a sour environment of arguments and ill-feeling for all to witness, resulting in Harrison walking out on 10 January and announcing he was leaving the Beatles. A week later his bandmates managed to woo him back by agreeing to his conditions – to record at the nicer, comfier Apple Studios in Savile Row, central London, and to find a role for the talented keyboard player Billy Preston, who the Beatles had known since their time in Hamburg and who George had watched perform with Ray Charles during his temporary period in absentia.

With Preston in situ as a calming influence, the atmosphere improved and the band continued rehearsing and recording with producer George Martin for several more days. On Sunday 26 January, someone (although who is not clear) came up with the brainwave of playing a live concert on the roof of the Apple Corps building as a way of finishing what had been elevated to a proper movie, not just a TV documentary. On Thursday 30 January at around lunchtime, the band headed to the roof to perform. After 42 minutes the celebrated concert was curtailed by the police, and the Beatles' last live performance was at an end. As a marketing concept it was a brilliant success but, once over, the 'Get Back' recordings were shelved and the band started work on their next album, *Abbey Road*. The only positive from the 'Get Back' sessions was the release of 'Get Back' as a single on 11 April 1969.

Nine months later, without consulting his bandmates, Lennon handed the 'Get Back' tapes over to the US record producer Phil Spector and asked him to make something from what he described as "the shittiest load of badly recorded shit". George Harrison and Ringo weren't too concerned, but George Martin was far from happy, while McCartney was furious and did his best to prevent Spector from going ahead with Lennon's instructions, but to no avail.

As George Martin commented in *The Beatles Anthology* book: "That made me angry – and it made Paul even angrier, because neither he nor I knew about it until it had been done. It happened behind our backs because it was done when Allen Klein was running John. He'd organised Phil Spector and I think George and Ringo had gone along with it."

With its new title, *Let it Be*, the Beatles' 12th and final studio album was released on 8 May 1970, a month after the Beatles had finally split; a rather dejected and morose finale to bring their spectacular career to an end.

So is the album *Let it Be* really as bad as McCartney and many others have suggested? Well, yes … and no. Spector had added excerpts of various studio discussions and applied orchestral and choir overdubs to four tracks: McCartney's 'The Long and Winding Road' and 'Let it Be', and to Harrison's 'I Me Mine'; he also messed with the album's loosely planned running order and removed 'Don't Let Me Down' (B-side of the 'Get Back' single) but included Lennon's 'Across the Universe' with additional piano, backing vocals, percussion and sound effects.

'Let it Be' or possibly 'Get Back' would have been the obvious opening track but Spector chose McCartney's pleasant ballad 'Two of Us', followed by Lennon's interesting 'Dig a Pony' and 'Across the Universe'. Harrison's equally decent 'I Me Mine' is then followed by a snatch of the 12-minute studio jam 'Dig It' (thankfully less than a minute long) before the title track, McCartney's hugely popular gospel creation, 'Let it Be'. With the traditional folk song concerning a Liverpool prostitute, 'Maggie Mae', finishing Side 1, Spector has basically sandwiched the album's classic number between two rather uninspiring tracks that shouldn't really have been included.

The running order for Side 2 is also questionable but there aren't really any bad songs. Even 'One After 909', a simple blues number, which Lennon and McCartney wrote back in 1963, had its nostalgic charm. And there are a couple of excellent numbers – McCartney's dreamy ballad 'The Long and Winding Road' and the classic rocker, 'Get Back'.

Truth is, the more you listen to *Let it Be*, the less you'll dislike it, if indeed you ever did. It's not a bad album but just overall lacks the cohesion, energy and inimitable Beatles vibe that most of their previous albums possessed – especially *Abbey Road* which, released just eight months earlier, was the Beatles' genuine swansong.

It should be remembered, however, that *Let it Be* is, officially, the Beatles' final LP and, for that reason alone, deserves to be treated with a little more respect. From a variety of fans, journalists, writers and perhaps even one or two Beatles as well, that has not always been the case.

LET IT BE... NAKED

Released:	17 November 2003
Label:	Apple
Producer:	Paul Hicks, Guy Massey and Allan Rouse
Recorded:	Apple Corps roof and Apple, EMI and Twickenham Film Studios, London
UK:	No. 7
USA:	No. 5

Side 1:
1. Get Back
2. Dig a Pony
3. For You Blue (Harrison)
4. The Long and Winding Road
5. Two of Us
6. I've Got a Feeling

Side 2:
1. One After 909
2. Don't Let Me Down
3. I Me Mine (Harrison)
4. Across the Universe
6. Let it Be

Let It Be... Naked is the alternative mix of Let it Be initiated by McCartney who, like many, felt that Phil Spector's version did not represent the band's original vision of the LP as a raw, back to the bones, rock 'n' roll album. While the other three Beatles were reasonably content, McCartney was furious with Spector's renowned 'Wall of Sound' production values, particularly on 'The Long and Winding Road', which Paul felt had been ravaged by the addition of orchestral and choral overdubs. Let it Be... Naked is made up of remixes of the original tracks but minus the studio chat and most of Phil Spector's overblown orchestral additions on the four tracks mentioned above. Two tracks – 'Dig It' and the traditional folk song 'Maggie Mae' – are omitted and replaced with 'Don't Let Me Down', the B-side on the single 'Get Back'. An additional 7-inch bonus disc contains song excerpts and dialogue as the Beatles rehearse and record during the filmed Let it Be sessions.

Opinions concerning whether or not Naked was a valid, worthwhile project vary considerably. Many agree that 'The Long and Winding Road' and 'Across the Universe' are preferable without Spector's strangulating strings and effects. Differences between the two 'Let it Be' mixes are minimal. While Harrison's 'I Me Mine' possibly sounds better on the original LP with Spector's added brass. Some believe the album Let it Be was what it was, and is what it is, and should be let it be. Each to their own.

LIVE ALBUMS

"I thought we were the best fucking group in the goddamn world and believing that is what made us what we were."

John Lennon

LIVE AT THE STAR-CLUB IN HAMBURG, GERMANY: 1962

Released: **8 April 1977**
Label: **Lingasong/Bellaphon (UK) and Lingasong/Atlantic (USA)**
Producer: **Larry Grossberg**
Recorded: **Star-Club, Hamburg**
UK: **Did not chart**
USA: **Did not chart**

Side 1:

1. **Introduction/I Saw Her Standing There** [US version: 'I'm Gonna Sit Right Down and Cry Over You' (Biggs-Thomas)]
2. **Roll Over Beethoven** (Berry)
3. **Hippy Hippy Shake** (Romero)
4. **Sweet Little Sixteen** (Berry)
5. **Lend Me Your Comb** (Twomey-Wise-Weisman)
6. **Your Feet's Too Big** (Benson-Fisher)

Side 2:

1. **Twist and Shout** (Medley-Russell) [US version: 'Where Have You Been (All My Life)' (Mann-Weil)]
2. **Mr. Moonlight** (Johnson)
3. **A Taste of Honey** (Scott-Marlow)
4. **Bésame Mucho** (Velázquez-Skylar)
5. **Reminiscing** (Curtis) [US version: 'Till There Was You' (Willson)]
6. **Kansas City/Hey-Hey-Hey-Hey/** (Leiber-Stoller/Penniman)

Side 3:

1. **Nothin' Shakin' (But the Leaves on the Trees)** (Fontaine-Colacrai-Lampert-Gluck)
2. **To Know Her is to Love Her** (Spector)
3. **Little Queenie** (Berry)
4. **Falling in Love Again (Can't Help It)** (Hollander-Lerner)
5. **Ask Me Why** [US version: 'Sheila' (Roe)]
6. **Be-Bop-A-Lula** (Vincent-Davis)
7. **Hallelujah I Love Her So** (Charles)

Side 4:

1. **Red Sails in the Sunset** (Kennedy-Williams)
2. **Everybody's Trying to Be My Baby** (Perkins)
3. **Matchbox** (Perkins)
4. **I'm Talking About You** (Berry)
5. **Shimmy Like Kate** (Piron-Smith-Goldsmith)
6. **Long Tall Sally** (Johnson-Penniman-Blackwell)
7. **I Remember You** (Mercer-Schertzinger)

This won't be everybody's cup of tea because the audio quality is not great (how could it be when it was captured on a mono reel-to-reel tape recorder placed at the front of the stage), but it's remarkable as a rare historic recording of the classic Beatles line-up playing for over an hour. There are only two of their own songs on the UK version but none on the US equivalent, which replaces four tracks with four other covers. These were the days when the Beatles were a good covers band on the cusp of hitting the big time. And doesn't it show.

THE BEATLES AT THE HOLLYWOOD BOWL

Released:	**4 May 1977**
Label:	**Parlophone (UK) and Capitol (USA)**
Producer:	**Voyle Gilmore and George Martin**
Recorded:	**Hollywood Bowl, Los Angeles**
UK:	**No. 1**
USA:	**No. 2**

Side 1:

1. **Twist and Shout** (Medley-Russell)
2. **She's a Woman**
3. **Dizzy Miss Lizzy** (Williams)
4. **Ticket to Ride**
5. **Can't Buy Me Love**
6. **Things We Said Today**
7. **Roll Over Beethoven** (Berry)

Side 2:

1. **Boys** (Dixon-Farrell)
2. **A Hard Day's Night**
3. **Help!**
4. **All My Loving**
5. **She Loves You**
6. **Long Tall Sally** (Johnson-Penniman-Blackwell)

LIVE AT THE HOLLYWOOD BOWL

Released:	**18 November 2016**
Label:	**Apple**
Producer:	**Voyle Gilmore, George Martin & Giles Martin**
Recorded:	**Hollywood Bowl, Los Angeles**
UK:	**No. 3**
USA:	**No. 7**

As above plus four additional tracks:

1. **You Can't Do That**
2. **I Want to Hold Your Hand**
3. **Everybody's Trying to Be My Baby** (Perkins)
4. **Baby's in Black**

Recorded at two Beatles concerts at the Hollywood Bowl during US tours in 1964 and '65 at the peak of Beatlemania, this is another important historic recording of exactly how crazy things were for the Fab Four by that stage; four young men playing electric guitars and a set of drums through a rather puny PA system up against almost 20,000 teenage screams. No contest. Little wonder the Beatles had had enough. But George Martin worked wonders to make Voyle Gilmore's original recordings actually listenable. And very touching that George's son, Giles, was able to improve the audio quality still further for a remastered version (plus four more additional tracks) to coincide with the *Eight Days a Week* motion picture released in 2016. George Martin died in March of that year so one can only hope that he was able to see and hear the results before he passed away.

LIVE ALBUMS

BELOW: Ticket for the 64 & 65 Hollywood Bowl gigs + The Beatles' perform at the Hollywood Bowl on August 23, 1964 in Los Angeles, California

THE BEATLES ON VINYL

THE BEATLES LIVE AT THE BBC

Released:	30 November 1994
Label:	Apple
Producer:	George Martin
Recorded:	Various BBC locations in London and Manchester
UK:	No. 1
USA:	No. 3

Side 1:

1. *Beatle Greetings*
2. From Us to You
3. *Riding on a Bus*
4. I Got a Woman (Charles)
5. Too Much Monkey Business (Berry)
6. Keep Your Hands Off My Baby (Goffin-King)
7. I'll Be on My Way
8. Young Blood (Leiber-Stoller-Pomus)
9. A Shot of Rhythm and Blues (Thompson)
10. Sure to Fall (In Love With You) (Perkins-Claunch-Cantrell)
11. Some Other Guy (Leiber-Stoller-Barrett)
12. Thank You Girl

Side 2:

1. *Sha La La La La!*
2. Baby it's You (David-Bacharach-Williams)
3. That's Alright (Mama) (Crudup)
4. Carol (Berry)
5. Soldier of Love (Cason-Moon)
6. *A Little Rhyme*
7. Clarabella (Pingatore)
8. I'm Gonna Sit Right Down and Cry (Over You) (Thomas-Biggs)
9. Crying, Waiting, Hoping (Holly)
10. *Dear Wack!*
11. You Really Got a Hold on Me (Robinson)

Side 3:

1. To Know Her is to Love Her (Spector)
2. A Taste of Honey (Marlow-Scott)
3. Long Tall Sally (Johnson-Penniman-Blackwell)
4. I Saw Her Standing There
5. The Honeymoon Song (Theodorakis-Sansom)
6. Johnny B. Goode (Berry)
7. Memphis, Tennessee (Berry)
8. Lucille (Collins-Penniman)
9. Can't Buy Me Love
10. *From Fluff to You*
11. Till There Was You (Willson)

Side 4:

1. *Crinsk Dee Night*
2. A Hard Day's Night
3. *Have a Banana!*
4. I Wanna Be Your Man
5. *Just a Rumour*
6. Roll Over Beethoven (Berry)
7. All My Loving
8. Things We Said Today
9. She's a Woman
10. Sweet Little Sixteen (Berry)
11. *1822!*
12. Lonesome Tears in My Eyes (J. and D. Burnette-Burlison-Mortimer)

RIGHT: Performing 'Paperback Writer' & 'Rain' on TOTP. 1966
FAR RIGHT: BBC recording at The Scala Theatre, London. 31st March 1964

LIVE ALBUMS

Side 5:

1. Nothin' Shakin' (Fontaine-Calacrai-Lampert-Gluck)
2. The Hippy Hippy Shake (Romero)
3. Glad All Over (Bennett-Tepper-Schroeder)
4. I Just Don't Understand (Wilkin-Westberry)
5. So How Come (No-One Loves Me) (Bryant)
6. I Feel Fine
7. I'm a Loser
8. Everybody's Trying to Be My Baby (Perkins)
9. Rock and Roll Music (Berry)
10. Ticket to Ride

Side 6:

1. Dizzy Miss Lizzy (Williams)
2. Kansas City/Hey-Hey-Hey-Hey (Leiber-Stoller/Penniman)
3. *Set Fire to That Lot!*
4. Matchbox (Perkins)
5. I Forgot to Remember to Forget (Kesler-Feathers)
6. *Love These Goon Shows!*
7. I Got to Find My Baby (Berry)
8. Ooh! My Soul (Penniman)
9. *Ooh! My Arms*
10. Don't Ever Change (Goffin-King)
11. Slow Down (Williams)
12. Honey Don't (Perkins)
13. Love Me Do

✶ Speech tracks in italics

Originally released in 1994 on CD and as a double-LP, but re-mastered and reissued as a triple-LP in 2013, this BBC collection combines many of the Beatles' hits plus a stockpile of 30 songs that were performed on air but never released on record in the Sixties. Selected from the band's 52 BBC radio performances on such regular shows as *Saturday Club* presented by Brian Matthew (who went on to present the BBC's *Sounds of the '60s* on Saturday mornings until 2017) and their own weekly show called *Pop Go the Beatles*. Highlights include a rare performance of the little known Lennon-McCartney composition 'I'll Be On My Way', plus a wide range of covers from the late Fifties and early Sixties. At the time of its release, *Live at the BBC* received very mixed reviews – some regarding it as rather "quaint" or "tame", while others saw it as an important musical "time capsule". *Rolling Stone* magazine was more appreciative, recognising the "irresistible spirit and energy of the performances". It was nominated for a Grammy Award for Best Historical Album in 1996.

ON AIR: LIVE AT THE BBC VOLUME 2

Released:	**25 November 2013**
Label:	**Apple**
Producer:	**Kevin Howlett, Mike Heatley, Jeff Jones**
Recorded:	**Various BBC locations in London and Manchester**
UK:	**No. 12**
USA:	**No. 7**

Released in 2013 (and reissued in 2017) as a triple vinyl LP companion to the Beatles' first BBC collection above, *On Air – Live at the BBC Volume 2* offers much of the same but with considerably more conversation pieces. It includes 37 previously unreleased performances and 23 previously unreleased recordings of in-studio conversations with BBC radio presenters Brian Matthews and Alan Freeman and *Pop Go The Beatles* hosts Lee Peters and Rodney Burke. Brian Matthew also conducts in-depth individual interviews with each of the four band members. Ten of the songs were never recorded by the Beatles for EMI in the Sixties, including debut performances of Chuck Berry's 'I'm Talking About You' and the old standard, 'Beautiful Dreamer'. Most of the Beatles' numbers are taken from their first four albums.

Side 1:

1. *And Here We Are Again*
2. **Words Of Love** (Holly)
3. *How About It, Gorgeous?*
4. **Do You Want To Know A Secret**
5. **Lucille** (Collins-Penniman)
6. *Hey, Paul...*
7. **Anna (Go to Him)** (Alexander)
8. *Hello!*
9. **Please Please Me**
10. **Misery**
11. **I'm Talking About You** (Berry)
12. *A Real Treat*
13. **Boys** (Dixon-Farrell)
14. *Absolutely Fab*
15. **Chains** (Goffin-King)
16. **Ask Me Why**

Side 2:

1. **Till There Was You** (Willson)
2. **Lend Me Your Comb** (Twomey-Wise-Weisman)
3. *Lower 5E*
4. **The Hippy Hippy Shake** (Romero)
5. **Roll Over Beethoven** (Berry)
6. **There's a Place**
7. *Bumper Bundle*
8. **P. S. I Love You**
9. **Please Mister Postman** (Dobbins-Garrett-Holland-Bateman)
10. **Beautiful Dreamer** (Foster-New)
11. **Devil in Her Heart** (Drapkin)
12. *The 49 Weeks*
13. **Sure to Fall (In Love With You)** (Perkins-Claunch-Cantrell)
14. *Never Mind, Eh?*
15. **Twist and Shout** (Medley-Russell)
16. *Bye, Bye*

RIGHT: *Recording the BBC radio programme 'Easy Beat'. October, 1963*

LIVE ALBUMS

Side 3:

1. I Saw Her Standing There
2. Glad All Over (Bennett-Tepper-Schroeder)
3. *Lift Lid Again*
4. I'll Get You
5. She Loves You
6. Memphis, Tennessee (Berry)
7. Happy Birthday Dear Saturday Club (Hill-Hill)
8. *Now Hush, Hush*
9. From Me to You
10. Money (That's What I Want) (Bradford-Gordy)
11. I Want to Hold Your Hand
12. *Brian Bathtubes*
13. This Boy
14. *If I Wasn't In America*

Side 4:

1. I Got A Woman (Charles-Richard)
2. Long Tall Sally (Johnson-Penniman-Blackwell)
3. If I Fell
4. *A Hard Job Writing Them*
5. And I Love Her
6. *Oh, Can't We? Yes We Can*
7. You Can't Do That
8. Honey Don't (Perkins)
9. I'll Follow The Sun
10. *Green With Black Shutters*
11. Kansas City /Hey-Hey-Hey-Hey (Leiber-Stoller/Penniman)
12. *That's What We're Here For*
13. I Feel Fine (studio out take)

Side 5:

1. *John – Pop Profile*
2. *George – Pop Profile*

Side 6:

1. *Paul – Pop Profile*
2. *Ringo – Pop Profile*

* Speech tracks in italics

THE BEATLES BROADCASTING CORPORATION: BEATLES NIGHT 7TH DECEMBER 1963

Released:	2017
Label:	London Calling
Producer:	Unknown
Recorded:	Empire Theatre, Liverpool
UK:	Did not chart
USA:	Did not chart

Side 1: Juke Box Jury

1. Hit and Miss (Barry)
2. Introduction by David Jacobs
3. I Could Write a Book (Rodgers-Hart) by the Chants
4. Kiss Me Quick (Pomus-Shuman) by Elvis Presley
5. Hippy Hippy Shake (Romero) by the Swinging Blue Jeans
6. Did You Have a Happy Birthday (Greenfield-Anka) by Paul Anka
7. The Nitty Gritty (Chase) by Shirley Ellis
8. I Can't Stop Talking About You (King-Goffin) by Steve & Eydie
9. Do You Really Love Me Too (Barkan-Raleigh) by Billy Fury
10. There I've Said it Again (Evans-Mann) by Bobby Vinton
11. Love Hit Me (Talmy) by the Orchids
12. I Think of You (Stirling) by the Merseybeats
13. Hit and Miss (reprise – Barry)

Side 2: Live at Empire Theatre, Liverpool

1. From Me to You
2. I Saw Her Standing There
3. All My Loving
4. Roll Over Beethoven (Berry)
5. Boys (Dixon-Farrell)
6. Till There Was You (Willson)
7. She Loves You
8. This Boy
9. I Want to Hold Your Hand
10. Money (That's What I Want) (Bradford-Gordy)
11. Twist and Shout (Medley-Russell)

Juke Box Jury was a very popular BBC TV show from 1959 to 1967 (based on an American show *Jukebox Jury*), on which celebrity guests would be asked to review the latest record releases and vote them either a hit, or a miss. John Lennon had already appeared as a guest in June 1963 but the Beatles were the first band to be invited as the entire panel at a special edition of *JBJ* in front of their Northern Area Fan Club Convention. The average weekly TV audience of 12 million viewers rose to 23 million to hear the Fab Four express their opinions on 13 new records (only 10 were broadcast) in their usual high-spirited and humorous way. Once the programme had finished, the Beatles played a live show for 2500 screaming fan club members, which was also recorded and broadcast on the BBC that evening. The sound quality is not brilliant (for example, Ringo's vocals on 'Boys' are inaudible) but worth a listen for an example of the level of energy at a Beatles show, especially in their hometown. Once finished, the band headed to Liverpool's Odeon Cinema for two more performances that night.

RIGHT: *The Beatles appear on the television programme Juke Box Jury in Liverpool with host David Jacobs, 7th December 1963*

LIVE ALBUMS

COMPILATION ALBUMS

"The Beatles will go on and on, on those records and films and videos and books and whatever, and in people's memories. It's become its own thing now. And the Beatles, I think, exist without us."

George Harrison MBE

A COLLECTION OF BEATLES OLDIES

With the band busy working on *Sgt. Pepper*, Parlophone needed to put something out there for the Christmas market, so this – their first and rather good compilation – was the result. Thirteen No. 1 hits plus 'Yesterday', 'Michelle' and Larry Williams classic blues rocker 'Bad Boy', previously unreleased in the UK. A terrific Sixties psychedelic cover, too, painted by the artist David Christian.

Released: **10 December 1966**
Label: **Parlophone**
Producer: **George Martin**
Recorded: **EMI Studios, London and Pathé Marconi Studios, Paris**
UK: **No. 7**
USA: **Not released**

Side 1:
1. She Loves You
2. From Me To You
3. We Can Work It Out
4. Help!
5. Michelle
6. Yesterday
7. I Feel Fine
8. Yellow Submarine

Side 2:
1. Can't Buy Me Love
2. Bad Boy (Williams)
3. Day Tripper
4. A Hard Days Night
5. Ticket To Ride
6. Paperback Writer
7. Eleanor Rigby
8. I Want To Hold Your Hand

HEY JUDE

Often regarded as a US Beatles album but actually just a compilation put together under instructions from the band's manager Allen Klein to fulfill the contract he had negotiated with Capitol Records. It features Beatles songs that hadn't appeared on US albums from 1964-69. Wasn't released in the UK but was readily available as an import. Album cover images by Linda McCartney at John Lennon's home, Tittenhurst Park in Berkshire.

Released: **26 February 1970**
Label: **Apple and Capitol**
Producer: **George Martin**
Recorded: **EMI, Apple and Trident Studios, London, and Pathé Marconi Studios, Paris**
UK: **Not released**
USA: **No. 2**

Side 1:
1. Can't Buy Me Love
2. I Should Have Known Better
3. Paperback Writer
4. Rain
5. Lady Madonna
6. Revolution

Side 2:
1. Hey Jude
2. Old Brown Shoe (Harrison)
3. Don't Let Me Down
4. The Ballad of John and Yoko

1962-1966 (RED ALBUM)

Put together by Beatles manager Allen Klein as part of a double-double-album collection of their greatest hits, this and its companion album 1967-70 were conceived as a way to limit sales of bootleg compilations that had been appearing from time to time. One of Angus McBean's 1963 Manchester Square photo shoot images for *Please Please Me* is dusted off. A great starting point for anyone out there who doesn't own a Beatles album, along with…

Released: **2 April 1973**
Label: **Apple**
Producer: **George Martin**
Recorded: **EMI Studios, London and Pathé Marconi Studios, Paris**
UK: **No. 3**
USA: **No. 3**

Side 1:
1. Love Me Do
2. Please Please Me
3. From Me to You
4. She Loves You
5. I Want to Hold Your Hand
6. All My Loving
7. Can't Buy Me Love

Side 2:
1. A Hard Day's Night
2. And I Love Her
3. Eight Days a Week
4. I Feel Fine
5. Ticket to Ride
6. Yesterday

Side 3:
1. Help!
2. You've Got to Hide Your Love Away
3. We Can Work it Out
4. Day Tripper
5. Drive My Car
6. Norwegian Wood (This Bird Has Flown)

Side 4:
1. Nowhere Man
2. Michelle
3. In My Life
4. Girl
5. Paperback Writer
6. Eleanor Rigby
7. Yellow Submarine

1967-1970 (BLUE ALBUM)

Obviously the second of the double-double collection and the slightly more popular of the two, as its chart positions indicate, which is hardly surprising when you consider the list of hit singles and cherry-picked tracks from their later Sixties albums. Almost 100 minutes of sheer brilliance. Front cover is Angus McBean's recreation of the 1963 shot at EMI's HQ in Manchester Square, taken in 1969.

Released: **2 April 1973**
Label: **Apple**
Producer: **George Martin and Phil Spector**
Recorded: **EMI, Olympic, Apple and Trident Studios, London**
UK: **No. 2**
USA: **No. 1**

Side 1:
1. Strawberry Fields Forever
2. Penny Lane
3. Sgt. Pepper's Lonely Hearts Club Band
4. With a Little Help from My Friends
5. Lucy in the Sky with Diamonds
6. A Day in the Life
7. All You Need Is Love

Side 2:
1. I Am the Walrus
2. Hello, Goodbye
3. The Fool on the Hill
4. Magical Mystery Tour
5. Lady Madonna
6. Hey Jude
7. Revolution

Side 3:
1. Back in the U.S.S.R.
2. While My Guitar Gently Weeps (Harrison)
3. Ob-La-Di, Ob-La-Da
4. Get Back
5. Don't Let Me Down
6. The Ballad of John and Yoko
7. Old Brown Shoe (Harrison)

Side 4:
1. Here Comes the Sun (Harrison)
2. Come Together
3. Something (Harrison)
4. Octopus's Garden (Starkey)
5. Let It Be
6. Across the Universe
7. The Long and Winding Road

LOVE SONGS

Another double-album compilation, loosely themed on love songs recorded by the Beatles between 1962-70. The gold-leaf style image on the front cover is based on a black and white portrait photographed by Richard Avedon, which is reproduced in full on the double gatefold covers.

Released: **21 October 1977 (USA)**
19 November 1977 (UK)
Label: **Capitol and Parlophone**
Producer: **George Martin & Phil Spector**
Recorded: **EMI, Olympic and Apple Studios, London**
UK: **No. 7**
USA: **No. 24**

Side 1:
1. Yesterday
2. I'll Follow the Sun
3. I Need You (Harrison)
4. Girl
5. In My Life
6. Words of Love (Holly)
7. Here, There and Everywhere

Side 2:
1. Something (Harrison)
2. And I Love Her
3. If I Fell
4. I'll Be Back
5. Tell Me What You See
6. Yes it Is

Side 3:
1. Michelle
2. It's Only Love
3. You're Going to Lose That Girl
4. Every Little Thing
5. For No One
6. She's Leaving Home

Side 2:
1. The Long and Winding Road
2. This Boy
3. Norwegian Wood (This Bird Has Flown)
4. You've Got to Hide Your Love Away
5. I Will
6. P.S. I Love You

RARITIES (UK)

Two similar versions of the same name but with very different songs – one for the UK market released in 1978 made up of B-sides and EP tracks, and the other for the USA market released 15 months later consisting of songs not readily available in the States. The UK version of Rarities was originally part of *The Beatles Collection* boxset released in the UK and USA in 1978 containing all 12 British LPs.

Released: **2 December 1978**
Label: **Parlophone**
Producer: **George Martin**
Recorded: **EMI Studios, London, Pathé Marconi Studios, Paris, and HMV Studios, Bombay**
UK: **No. 71**
USA: **Not Released**

COMPILATION ALBUMS

Side 1:
1. Across the Universe
2. Yes It Is
3. This Boy
4. **The Inner Light** (Harrison)
5. I'll Get You
6. Thank You Girl
7. Komm, Gib Mir Deine Hand (German 'I Want to Hold Your Hand')
8. You Know My Name (Look Up the Number)
9. Sie Liebt Dich (German 'She Loves You')

Side 2:
1. Rain
2. She's a Woman
3. **Matchbox** (Perkins)
4. I Call Your Name
5. **Bad Boy** (Williams)
6. **Slow Down** (Williams)
7. I'm Down
8. **Long Tall Sally** (Johnson-Penniman-Blackwell)

RARITIES (USA)

Released:	24 March 1980
Label:	Capitol
Producer:	George Martin
Recorded:	EMI Studios, London, Pathé Marconi Studios, Paris, and HMV Studios, Bombay
UK:	Not Released
USA:	No. 21

Side 1:
1. Love Me Do
2. Misery
3. There's a Place
4. Sie Liebt Dich (German 'She Loves You')
5. And I Love Her
6. Help!
7. I'm Only Sleeping
8. I Am the Walrus

Side 2:
1. Penny Lane
2. Helter Skelter
3. **Don't Pass Me By** (Starkey)
4. **The Inner Light** (Harrison)
5. Across the Universe
6. You Know My Name (Look Up the Number)
7. Sgt. Pepper Inner Groove

THE BEATLES BALLADS

A compilation of classic weepy ballads spanning 1964 to 1970, released just seven weeks before John Lennon was murdered in New York. Interesting cover painting from Scottish artist and writer, John Byrne, originally intended for a possible Beatles album's working title 'A Doll's House', which eventually became *The Beatles* 'White Album'.

Released: **13 October 1980**
Label: **Parlophone**
Producer: **George Martin**
Recorded: **EMI, Trident and Apple Studios, London**
UK: **No. 17**
USA: **Not released**

Side 1:

1. Yesterday
2. Norwegian Wood (This Bird Has Flown)
3. Do You Want to Know a Secret
4. For No One
5. Michelle
6. Nowhere Man
7. You've Got to Hide Your Love Away
8. Across the Universe
9. All My Loving
10. Hey Jude

Side 2:

1. Something (Harrison)
2. The Fool on the Hill
3. Till There Was You (Willson)
4. The Long and Winding Road
5. Here Comes the Sun (Harrison)
6. Blackbird
7. And I Love Her
8. She's Leaving Home
9. Here, There and Everywhere
10. Let It Be

20 GREATEST HITS

The UK compilation contained all 19 tracks from the Beatles' 17 No. 1 singles (including double A-sides), plus their very first single 'Love Me Do'. The US version replaced six of the UK hits with six No. 1s of their own. The US running order is also slightly different.

Released:	**11 October 1982 (USA)**
	18 October 1982 (UK)
Label:	**Capitol and Parlophone**
Producer:	**George Martin**
Recorded:	**EMI, Trident and Apple Studios, London and Pathé Marconi Studios, Paris**
UK:	**No. 10**
USA:	**No. 50**

Side 1:

1. Love Me Do
2. From Me to You

(Replaced with 'Eight Days a Week' on US version)

3. She Loves You
4. I Want to Hold Your Hand
5. Can't Buy Me Love
6. A Hard Day's Night
7. I Feel Fine
8. Ticket to Ride
9. Help!
10. Day Tripper

(Replaced with 'Yesterday' on US version)

11. We Can Work It Out

Side 2:

1. Paperback Writer
2. Yellow Submarine

(Replaced with 'Penny Lane' on US version)

3. Eleanor Rigby

(Replaced with 'Come Together' on US version)

4. All You Need is Love
5. Hello, Goodbye
6. Lady Madonna

(Replaced with 'Let it Be' on US version)

7. Hey Jude
8. Get Back
9. The Ballad of John and Yoko

(Replaced with 'The Long and Winding Road' on US version)

PAST MASTERS (VOLUMES ONE AND TWO VINYL VERSION)

Originally released in March 1988 as two separate CDs forming part of *The Beatles Box Set*, but subsequently as a vinyl double-album seven months later. Not really all that rare as most of the tracks are A-sides and B-sides of singles and four from the *Long Tall Sally* EP. But certainly worth considering if you only own the 12 UK studio albums.

Released: **24 October 1988 (US)**
10 November 1988 (UK)
Label: **Capitol, Parlophone and Apple**
Producer: **George Martin**
Recorded: **EMI, Olympic, Apple and Trident Studios, London, and Pathé Marconi Studios, Paris**
UK: **No. 49 and No. 46**
USA: **Did not chart**

Side 1:
1. Love Me Do
2. From Me to You
3. Thank You Girl
4. She Loves You
5. I'll Get You
6. I Want to Hold Your Hand
7. This Boy
8. Komm, Gib Mir Deine Hand (German 'I Want to Hold Your Hand')
9. Sie Liebt Dich (German 'She Loves You')

Side 2:
1. Long Tall Sally (Johnson-Penniman-Blackwell)
2. I Call Your Name
3. Slow Down (Williams)
4. Matchbox (Perkins)
5. I Feel Fine
6. She's a Woman
7. Bad Boy (Williams)
8. Yes It Is
9. I'm Down

Side 3:
1. Day Tripper
2. We Can Work It Out
3. Paperback Writer
4. Rain
5. Lady Madonna
6. The Inner Light (Harrison)
7. Hey Jude
8. Revolution

Side 4:
1. Get Back
2. Don't Let Me Down
3. The Ballad of John and Yoko (Dropped from Side 6 of *Mono Masters*)
4. Old Brown Shoe (Harrison) (Dropped from Side 6 of *Mono Masters*)
5. Across the Universe
6. Let It Be (Dropped from Side 6 of *Mono Masters*)
7. You Know My Name (Look Up the Number)

COMPILATION ALBUMS

MONO MASTERS (VINYL)

Same running order as above but the tracks are spread more evenly across six discs to improve hi-fi quality. As indicated, three tracks from *Past Masters* Side 4 have been dropped from *Mono Masters* as they were not available in mono. Side 5 of *Mono Masters* features four additional songs from *Yellow Submarine*:

Released:	**9 September 2014**
Label:	**Parlophone, Capitol and Apple**
Producer:	**George Martin**
Recorded:	**EMI, Olympic, Apple and Trident Studios, London, and Pathé Marconi Studios, Paris**
UK:	**Did not chart**
USA:	**Did not chart**

Side 5:
1. Only a Northern Song (Harrison)
2. All Together Now
3. Hey Bulldog
4. It's All Too Much (Harrison)

Mono Masters formed part of *The Beatles in Mono* box set released on CD in 2009, followed by a limited edition vinyl version in 2014 (see Boxsets section). *Mono Masters* is still available as an individual triple-album providing exceptional sound quality.

THE BEATLES ON VINYL

THE BEATLES
27 No. 1s
NEW STEREO MIXES

1

Presented chronologically, the 27 Beatles songs that went to No. 1 in the UK or USA. No surprise that they went straight back to No. 1 in both countries (and just about everywhere else) when originally released in 2000 on CD and vinyl. A re-mastered heavyweight version was put together by Giles Martin and released in 2015. A superb package apart from what appears to be a serious omission: 'Strawberry Fields Forever' was a double-A-side with 'Penny Lane', which made it to No. 1 in the USA. Why isn't it included? The answer is that, although 'Penny Lane' was a US No. 1, 'Strawberry Fields Forever' only made it to No. 8. Strange.

Released:	**13 November 2000**
Label:	**Capitol, Parlophone and Apple**
Producer:	**George Martin, Phil Spector and Giles Martin**
Recorded:	**EMI, Apple, Olympic and Trident Studios, London and Pathé Marconi Studios, Paris**
UK:	**No. 1**
USA:	**No. 1**

Side 1 (1962-64):
1. Love Me Do
2. From Me to You
3. She Loves You
4. I Want to Hold Your Hand
5. Can't Buy Me Love
6. A Hard Day's Night
7. I Feel Fine
8. Eight Days a Week

Side 2 (1965-66):
1. Ticket to Ride
2. Help!
3. Yesterday
4. Day Tripper
5. We Can Work it Out
6. Paperback Writer
7. Yellow Submarine
8. Eleanor Rigby

Side 3 (1967-68):
1. Penny Lane
2. All You Need is Love
3. Hello Goodbye
4. Lady Madonna
5. Hey Jude

Side 4 (1969-70):
1. Get Back
2. The Ballad of John and Yoko
3. Something (Harrison)
4. Come Together
5. Let it Be
6. The Long and Winding Road

LOVE

The story of what is, in effect, a soundtrack for a big circus show is extraordinary and could easily become a film within itself, with a soundtrack of a soundtrack. In a nutshell: George Harrison became friends with Guy Laliberté – the founder of Canada's Cirque du Soleil – at a Formula One race. Between them, they came up with the concept of *Love*, a musical based on the Beatles' story presented as a spectacular circus show in Las Vegas. It's the sort of idea that could have been shot down in flames when proposed but, despite George sadly dying in November 2001, his widow, Olivia Harrison, along with Yoko Ono, Paul and Ringo gave their approval for George Martin and his son Giles to come full circle and create a new Beatles album.

What they have achieved in re-mastering the original four- and eight-track analogue tapes as a Beatles songs mash-up is remarkable and, although not everyone approves or appreciates it, the recording went on to win two Grammys and, most importantly, the two remaining Beatles loved it. As Ringo said: "Really powerful… I even heard things I'd forgotten we'd recorded."

The show has toured the world and continues to be performed (although temporarily postponed during the Covid-19 pandemic in 2020/21) at the Mirage casino in Las Vegas twice a day, five days a week. Circus or not, the soundtrack is stunning. To experience some of the Beatles' best ever songs in a totally new way, *Love is all you need*.

Released:	**20 November 2006**
Label:	**Apple, Capitol and Parlophone**
Producer:	**George Martin / Giles Martin**
Recorded:	**EMI, Trident, Olympic and Apple Studios, London, EMI Studios, Bombay, and Hollywood Bowl, Los Angeles**
UK:	**No. 3**
USA:	**No. 4**

Side 1:
1. Because
2. Get Back
3. Glass Onion
4. Eleanor Rigby (with 'Julia' transition)
5. I Am the Walrus
6. I Want to Hold Your Hand
7. Drive My Car/The Word/What You're Doing
8. Gnik Nus ('Sun King' backwards)
9. Something (with 'Blue Jay Way' transition) (Harrison)

Side 2:
1. Being for the Benefit of Mr. Kite!/I Want You (She's So Heavy)/Helter Skelter
2. Help!
3. Blackbird/Yesterday
4. Strawberry Fields Forever
5. Within You Without You/Tomorrow Never Knows (Harrison/Lennon–McCartney)
6. Lucy in the Sky with Diamonds
7. Octopus's Garden (Starkey) (with 'Sun King' transition)

COMPILATION ALBUMS

Side 3:
1. Lady Madonna
2. Here Comes the Sun
(with 'The Inner Light' transition) (Harrison)
3. Come Together/Dear Prudence
(with 'Cry Baby Cry' transition)
4. Revolution
5. Back in the U.S.S.R.

Side 4:
1. While My Guitar Gently Weeps
(*Anthology 3* version) (Harrison)
2. A Day in the Life
3. Hey Jude
4. Sgt. Pepper's Lonely Hearts Club Band (Reprise)
5. All You Need Is Love

RECORD EIGHT

...ilation. ℗ 1980
...cords Ltd., U.K.

33 1/3 R.P.M.
R-91110
SW 10387

THE BEATLES BOX — THE BEATLES   1
1: GET BACK (Lennon-McCartney)
2: DON'T LET ME DOWN (Lennon-McCartney)
3: THE BALLAD OF JOHN AND YOKO
(Lennon-McCartney)
4: ACROSS THE UNIVERSE (Lennon-McCartney)
5: FOR YOU BLUE* (Harrison)
6: TWO OF US (Lennon-McCartney)
7: LONG AND WINDING ROAD
(Lennon-McCartney)
8: LET IT BE (Lennon-McCartney)
(All titles ATV Northern Songs, except
*Essex)

MADE IN AUSTRALIA BY E M I (AUSTRALIA) LIMITED

BOXSETS

THE BEATLES COLLECTION

Released: 2 November 1978 (US) and 12 December 1978 (UK)
Label: Capitol and Parlophone

A boxset of 12 Beatles UK stereo albums (*Magical Mystery Tour* is not included as it was not originally released in the UK) plus *Rarities* (see Compilations). Released for the UK and US markets, with the US version limited to 3000 numbered copies, which sold out within a few days.

THE BEATLES BOX

Released: 3 November 1980
Label: Parlophone and World Records

This eight-record boxset was available on mail-order from World Records – a subsidiary of EMI. Includes every Beatles UK single plus a selection of tracks from every UK album, plus *Magical Mystery Tour*.

THE BEATLES: THE COLLECTION (HALF-SPEED MASTERS)

Released: 1 October 1982
Label: Mobile Fidelity Sound Lab

A vinyl boxset of all of the Beatles UK albums (plus *Magical Mystery Tour*) re-mastered at half-speed from the original stereo master recordings and pressed in Japan by JVC. Released originally as a limited edition and renowned for its superb sound quality.

THE BEATLES MONO COLLECTION

Released: 3 October 1982
Label: Parlophone and Apple

All nine Beatles UK albums originally released in mono, from *Please Please Me* to *The Beatles* ('White Album'), plus *Yellow Submarine* which was converted to mono simply by combining two stereo channels into one. Available in a black box featuring repro silver print autographs from the four band members. Rumour has it that some UK copies were released in a red box, but thought to be less than 500 available. Either way, they're not particularly easy to find.

THE BEATLES ANTHOLOGY (VINYL VERSIONS)

ANTHOLOGY 1
Released: **20 November 1995**
Label: **Apple and Capitol**
UK: **2**
USA: **1**

ANTHOLOGY 2
Released: **18 March 1996**
Label: **Apple and Capitol**
UK: **1**
USA: **1**

ANTHOLOGY 3
Released: **28 October 1996**
Label: **Apple and Capitol**
UK: **4**
USA: **1**

Released as three triple-albums over 11 months from November 1995 to October 1996, *The Beatles Anthology* collection formed part of a project that also included a television documentary and DVD, plus a large format hardback book, all combining to present a history of the Beatles in more detail than ever before. Most would agree that none of the alternative recordings here are improvements on the finished items we have all lived with and listened to for many years, but they do offer a fascinating insight into the Beatles as individuals, as talented musicians and, along with George Martin and his sound engineers, their innovative approach to making the best of the limited technology available to them in the studio.

Anthology 1 covers the Beatles story from their early days as the Quarrymen, through their failed audition at Decca Records, live recordings in Hamburg, Stockholm, London and New York, and recording sessions for their first four albums with George Martin at EMI Studios. Opening track is the John Lennon song 'Free as a Bird', released as a single in December 1995.

Anthology 2 begins with a follow up single 'Real Love' released in March 1996 before recording sessions and alternative takes of various singles and tracks from the albums *Help!, Rubber Soul, Revolver, Sgt. Pepper's Lonely Hearts Club Band* plus the *Magical Mystery Tour* double-EP. There are also live performances in Blackpool, New York and Tokyo.

Anthology 3 includes several home recordings made by the Beatles at George Harrison's home in Esher, Surrey, running through songs that eventually appeared on the 'White Album', the infamous Savile Row sessions at Apple Studio for the film and LP, *Let it Be*, and EMI Studio sessions for their final recordings of the superb LP *Abbey Road*.

It's hard to know how to define *The Beatles Anthology* as albums – individual triple-LPs? Or a series of compilations? Or, as we like to think of it, as the definitive alternative Beatles boxset. The albums' covers – painted collages of various Beatles images, LP covers and posters by Klaus Voormann (responsible for the *Revolver* cover) and fellow German illustrator Alfons Kiefer – collected together, end-to-end, create the appearance of a wall of peeling posters and album covers that tell the Beatles' story from start to finish. These LPs simply belong together in this well-worth searching for, nine-disc, vinyl boxset.

THE BEATLES IN STEREO (VINYL VERSION)

Released: **12 November 2012**
Label: **Apple**

Originally released as a CD boxset in 2009, vinyl enthusiasts had to wait over three years for the 180-gram, audiophile quality vinyl versions of the 13 Beatles stereo albums (including the US *Magical Mystery Tour*) complete with replicated artwork and accompanied by the double-album *Past Masters*, plus a 252-page hardbound book. The stereo boxset had been conceived and produced so outstandingly well that it was an exciting moment for many vinyl collectors when it finally arrived. For the out-and-out purists, however, there were almost two more years of mouth-watering anticipation to get through until the arrival of…

THE BEATLES IN MONO (VINYL VERSION)

Released: **9 September 2014**
Label: **Apple**

Also originally released on CD in 2009, it was almost five years later before the much-anticipated, limited edition, heavyweight, 180-gram vinyl boxset re-mastered from the analogue tapes (rather than digitally), and launched at EMI Studios, Abbey Road, on 8 September 2014. In addition to the Beatles' 10 original mono LPs from *Please Please Me* to *The Beatles* ('White Album'), including *Magical Mystery Tour*, there's also the superb triple-album *Mono Masters*. The sound quality throughout is staggeringly good – well worth the cost if you've got a decent hi-fi system, but now not so easy to find.

The Beatles pose on a London rooftop, circa 1964

THE BEATLES' CHRISTMAS RECORDS

Released: **15 December 2017**
Label: **Apple**

Originally released from 1963 to 1969 on flexi-disk for the Beatles' official UK and US fan club members, seven titles were produced:

1963: *The Beatles Christmas Record* (produced by Tony Barrow)
1964: *Another Beatles Christmas Record* (produced by Tony Barrow)
1965: *The Beatles Third Christmas Record* (produced by Tony Barrow)
1966: *Pantomime: Everywhere it's Christmas* (produced by George Martin)
1967: *Christmas Time is Here Again!* (produced by George Martin)
1968: *The Beatles 1968 Christmas Record* (produced by Kenny Everett)
1969: *The Beatles Seventh Christmas Record* (produced by Kenny Everett)

When the band broke up in December 1970, the UK fan club sent out a compilation vinyl LP of all seven Christmas recordings, *From Then to You* (or *The Beatles Christmas Album* in the US), re-mastered from the original flexi discs as the master tapes had been lost. In 2017 Apple released the Christmas singles as a 7-inch vinyl boxset of all seven titles. Comes with a 16-page booklet containing the fan club's Christmas newsletters.

HOME AND AWAY '64-'66

Released: **2018**
Label: **Audio Visual Archive**

This 5-LP boxed set contains five re-mastered live performances using entire original national broadcasts from five venues around the world. Comes with a 60-page hardback book and an A2 colour poster. A more expensive coloured vinyl limited edition of 1000 copies is also available, but not so easy to find.

DISC 1:
Festival Hall, Melbourne, Australia,
17 June 1964 (National Television Network)

DISC 2:
ABC Theatre, Blackpool, England,
19 July 1964 (ITV Network)

DISC 3:
Philadelphia Convention Hall, USA,
2 September 1964 (WXPN)

DISC 4:
Palais Sports, Paris, France,
20 June 1965 (Europe 1)

DISC 5:
Budokan Hall, Tokyo, Japan,
30 June 1966 (NTV Channel 4)

RIGHT: *The Beatles celebrate Christmas, 1964*

...rights of the Manufacturer and of the Owner of the recorded work reserved

PARLOPHONE

TRADE MARK

MADE IN GT BRITAIN

45-R 4949
MONO

LOVE ME DO
(Lennon–McCartney)
THE BEATLES

...performance, broadcasting and copying of this record prohibited

SINGLES

THE BEATLES ON VINYL

1962

Love Me Do/P.S. I Love You

Released UK:	5 October 1962 on Parlophone
Released USA:	27 April 1964 on Tollie (subsidiary of Vee-Jay)
UK:	17
USA:	1

George Martin selected this as the Beatles' first single for Parlophone mainly because he liked John Lennon's harmonica sound. He wasn't so keen on Ringo's drumming during the first recording session and brought in session drummer Andy White while Ringo played tambourine. He wasn't happy. In the end, Ringo's drumming was retained for the single, while Andy's was used for the *Please Please Me* LP version. Either way, a simple, largely two-chord pop song with a great hook that entered the public's subconscious for weeks (years?) to come. It wasn't released in the USA until after the Beatles' success in 1963/64 but did make it No. 1 more than 18 months after the UK release.

1963

Please Please Me/Ask Me Why

Released UK:	11 January 1963 on Parlophone
Released USA:	25 February 1963 on Vee-Jay
UK:	2
USA:	**Did not chart**

'Please Please Me' was composed by John at home at his Aunt Mimi's house originally as a slow ballad, but George Martin recognised immediately that it needed "pepping up …it was very slow and rather dreary," he said. "I told them if they doubled the speed it might be interesting." As usual, he was right. And so convinced was he that, towards the end of the recording session, he announced, "You've just made your first No.1." Almost right. It only made it to No. 2 in the UK's Official Chart and eventually to No. 3 in the US Billboard Hot 100 when it was re-released by Vee-Jay in January 1964 with 'From Me to You' on the B-side.

From Me To You/Thank You Girl

Released UK:	11 April 1963 on Parlophone
Released USA:	27 May 1963 on Vee-Jay
UK:	1
USA:	Did not chart

'From Me To You', was written by John and Paul while taking part in the Helen Shapiro national package tour, driving up and down the country in the back of a cramped little van. Probably not the ideal location to write a love song. Most would agree that it's not one of their best, but catchy as always, with a hooky harmonica intro. Made it to No.1 in the UK but only No. 116 in the US, just outside the Hot 100.
The B-side 'Thank You Girl' is certainly not one of their best; rather dreary and doesn't even sound like the Beatles.

She Loves You/I'll Get You

Released UK:	23 August 1963 on Parlophone
Released USA:	16 September 1963 on Swan Records
UK:	1
USA:	1

A song that John and Paul began in a Newcastle hotel room and finished a few days later at Paul's family home in Liverpool, this was the record that became the best-selling single of the Sixties. "Yeah, yeah, yeah!" Everyone loved it but Paul's dad wasn't too keen on the American pronunciation. "Couldn't you sing: 'She loves you. Yes! Yes! Yes!'?" he asked politely. Similarly, George Martin wasn't too keen on the jazzy sixth chord the Beatles insisted on closing the song with. "Too jazzy," said Martin. "A great hook," responded the three guitarists. Ending (or starting) a song with a hook chord was something the Beatles became masters of.

THE BEATLES ON VINYL

I Want To Hold Your Hand/This Boy
Released UK: 29 November 1963 on Parlophone

I Want To Hold Your Hand/I Saw Her Standing There
Released USA: 26 December 1963 on Capitol
UK: 1
USA: 1

If 'She Loves You' was the song that broke the Beatles in the UK, then 'I Want to Hold Your Hand', written at Jane Asher's parents' house in London, was the one that exported their fame and talent around the world. Despite their previous reluctance, Capitol Records had to sit up and take notice at last, and were glad they had. Playing it live on *The Ed Sullivan Show* on 9 February 1964 has repeatedly been referred to as a pivotal moment in US culture; sounds pretentious, but it's true. Beatlemania and the British invasion had arrived.

1964

Twist and Shout (Medley-Russell)/There's a Place
Released USA: 2 March 1964 on Tollie
UK: Not released
USA: 23

Another example of Vee-Jay or one of its subsidiaries taking advantage of their five-year option on Beatles singles while the legal battle with Capitol dragged on. Both taken from the *Please Please Me* LP and the Beatles' first UK EP *Twist and Shout* released by Parlophone in July 1963, which sold more than 750,000 copies.

SINGLES

Can't Buy Me Love/You Can't Do That

Released UK:	20 March 1964 on Parlophone
Released USA:	16 March 1963 on Capitol
UK:	1
USA:	1

Returning from their incredibly successful first American tour, the Beatles returned to the UK superheroes and prepared to make their first movie, *A Hard Day's Night*. The initial single from the soundtrack had been written and recorded in Paris because the band had a near three-week residency at the Olympia concert venue, playing often two or three times a day, so it made sense for George Martin to fly over from London, rather than vice versa. Fun, bouncy, heavily jazz-influenced, this was the single that everyone seemed to love, from teenagers to grandparents.

Do You Want to Know a Secret?/Thank You Girl

Released USA:	23 March 1964 on Vee-Jay
UK:	Not released
USA:	2

Vee-Jay's fifth and final Beatles single, backed with the rather disappointing B-side previously mentioned, 'Thank You Girl'.

A Hard Day's Night/Things We Said Today

Released UK: 10 July 1964 on Parlophone

A Hard Day's Night/I Should Have Known Better

Released USA:	13 July 1964 on Capitol
UK:	1
USA:	1

Everyone knows that opening guitar chord, even if really clever musicologists seem to be unable to agree what it is. People have written academic papers on it, but still there's no definite decision on exactly how it was played. None of the band members or George Martin seem to remember, either. The truth is, it's more than just a guitar chord:

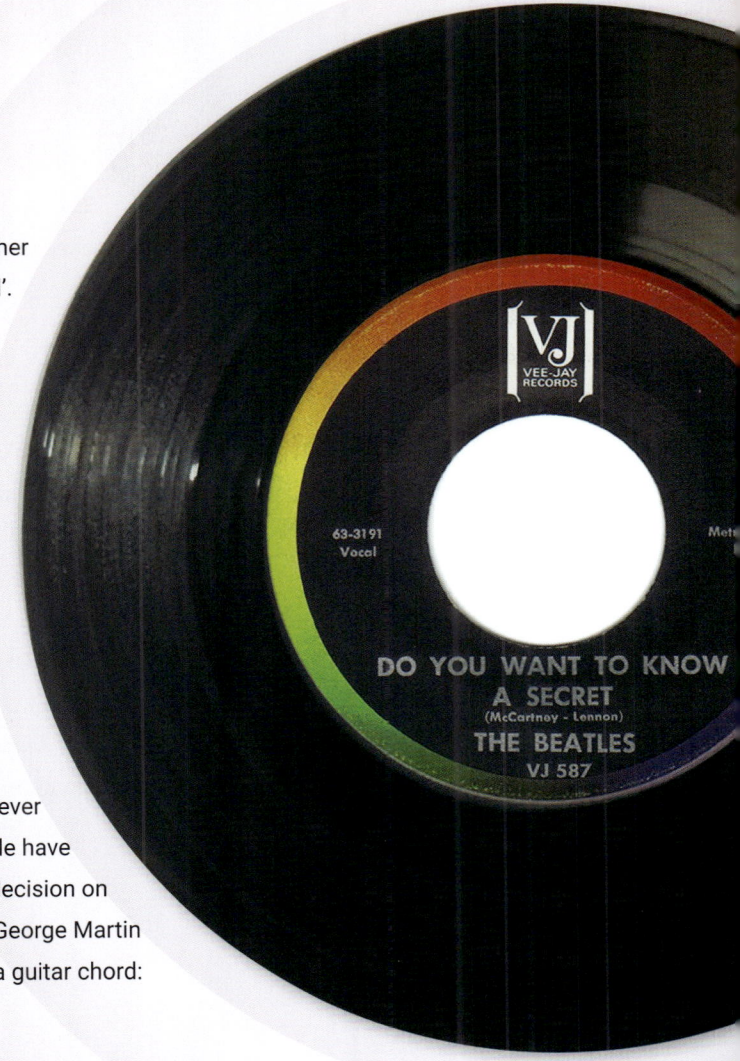

THE BEATLES ON VINYL

Harrison is playing a 12-string electric; Lennon a 6-string acoustic; McCartney on bass; George Martin on grand piano; and Ringo's somewhere in there, too, playing a snare drum and cymbal. It's a case of several disconnected things all coming together and reacting with one another harmonically to create something rather wonderful that really shouldn't sound like that at all. Musical combobulation. Anyway, it's now one of the most famous intros in rock. And the other two and a half minutes aren't bad either. Best just to listen.

I'll Cry Instead/I'm Happy Just to Dance With You

Released USA:	20 July 1964 on Capitol
UK:	Not released
USA:	25

And I Love Her/If I Fell

Released USA:	20 July 1964 on Capitol
UK:	Not released
USA:	12

Matchbox (Perkins)/Slow Down (Williams)

Released USA:	24 August 1964 on Capitol
UK:	Not released
USA:	17

A series of three singles released in the USA by Capitol over a short space of time – two from *A Hard Day's Night* released on the same day, and one a month later from the very similar *Something New* LP. The last of the three was the only single the Beatles ever released with neither of the songs written by band members. All were big fans of Carl Perkins and would perform 'Matchbox' live in the early days with the vocals handled by original drummer Pete Best.

I Feel Fine/She's a Woman

Released UK:	**27 November 1964 on Parlophone**
Released USA:	**23 November 1964 on Capitol**
UK:	**1**
USA:	**1**

Despite the run of singles lifted from the *A Hard Day's Night* LP, the Beatles still preferred standalone singles and chose this as the last one for 1964. It was also the first Beatles single to feature fuzzy feedback in another interesting chord opening and a brilliant guitar riff written by John but performed by George Harrison virtually from start to finish. According to Harrison it was Lennon who came up with the idea to use the guitar feedback for the song's opening (combined with a single sustained note on McCartney's bass), when he unintentionally leaned his semi-acoustic guitar against an amplifier. He liked the sound and decided to try to reproduce it on every take. Nor should this single's flipside, 'She's a Woman', be allowed to go short of praise. A superb Little Richard R&B pastiche written largely by McCartney. At three minutes long, it's probably the best Beatles B-side so far.

1965

Eight Days a Week/I Don't Want to Spoil the Party

Released USA:	**15 February 1965 on Capitol**
UK:	**Not released**
USA:	**1**

Both tracks taken from the UK *Beatles for Sale* and equivalent US *Beatles VI* LPs. The A-side title is said to have been based on a comment made by a chauffer driving Paul McCartney to John Lennon's house in Surrey. When McCartney asked him how he was, the chauffer replied, "Working hard – eight days a week." Excellent track known for its opening guitar and bass fade-in technique not known to have been used before. Lennon's B-side is another fine country-and-western ditty about a young man who's been stood up by his girlfriend at a party, with an excellent Carl Perkins guitar solo from Harrison.

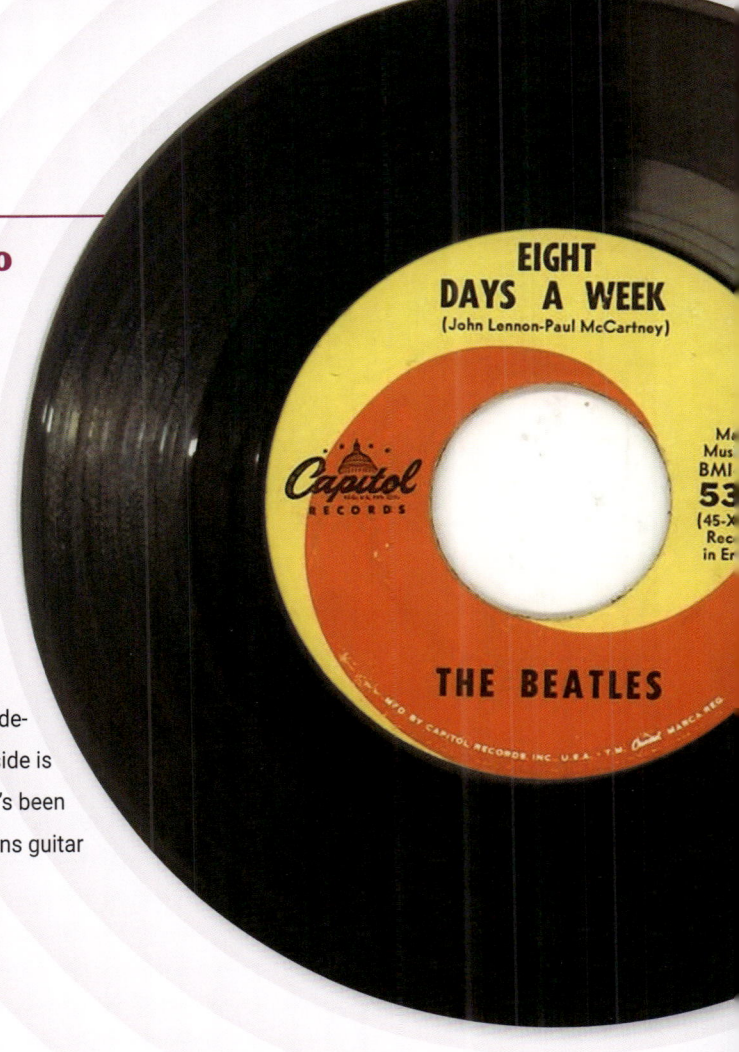

Ticket To Ride/Yes it Is

Released UK:	**9 April 1965 on Parlophone**
Released USA:	**19 April 1965 on Capitol**
UK:	**1**
USA:	**1**

With its jangly Rickenbacker guitars and Ringo's excellent rhythmic tom-toms, this is not the first Beatles recording that immediately stirs images of the Byrds and California sunshine, but it's one of, if not the, very best. This was the record that demonstrated George Martin's decision to hand over more studio control to the boys themselves, and it paid dividends. "I could recognise that any idea coming from them was better than an idea coming from me," he said. Droning guitars, strange drumming patterns, tempo changes… this was a new, radical sound for the Beatles. Some also believe this is the Beatles' first drug-influenced record after LSD experimentation a few weeks before. Who knows? Whatever, it worked brilliantly. B-side is in complete contrast: 'Yes it Is', a simple love song from Lennon in a similar vein to 'This Boy'.

Help!/I'm Down

Released UK:	**23 July 1965 on Parlophone**
Released USA:	**19 July 1965 on Capitol**
UK:	**1**
USA:	**1**

The Beatles were movie stars for the second time early in 1965 when they started filming *Help!*, with shooting taking place in the Bahamas in February, followed by snow scenes in Obertauern, Austria. Sounds fun, but the Beatles were often bored, which sometimes resulted in them enjoying themselves too much. In *The Beatles Anthology* McCartney says that much of their time was spent smoking joints and lying, laughing helplessly, on the sand or in the snow. But 'helpless', it transpired, was exactly how Lennon was feeling. "I just wrote the song because I was commissioned to write it for the movie – but later I knew, really I was crying out for help. 'Help!' was about me." The B-side, 'I'm Down', didn't reflect Lennon's state of mind but was written by McCartney as another Little Richard pastiche, featuring some excellent Vox Continental keyboards provided by John.

Yesterday/Act Naturally (Russell)

Released USA: **13 September 1965 on Capitol**
UK: **Not released**
USA: **1**

Hard to believe that 'Yesterday' wasn't released as a single in the UK until 1976, which doesn't really count. The Beatles were long gone by then. It was released as the title track on an EP in 1966, but apparently the other three band members weren't keen on it being released as a single because it was really a McCartney solo performance, apart from a string quartet accompanying him. Not a great business decision for a record that went on to win more 'best song' polls and become the most covered title in the history of recorded music. Put it this way: if this had been the only song McCartney ever wrote, he'd still be a wealthy man. But such were everyone's doubts about it at the time, including Paul's, that it was originally offered to Chris Farlowe… who turned it down! Just as well, as the version he did record the following year was pretty turgid. The B-side is one of Ringo's few vocal performances on a single – the nice country-and-western song written by Johnny Russell, 'Act Naturally', that had been a US hit for Buck Owens in 1963.

We Can Work It Out/Day Tripper

Released UK: **3 December 1965 on Parlophone**
Released USA: **3 December 1965 on Capitol**
UK: **1**
USA: **1**

Despite, or maybe because of, Lennon's mental health issues, he was definitely on a roll in terms of writing hit songs. Of the Beatles' last five A-sides, Lennon had been the major composer on no less than four of them. Here was their first double-A-sided single on which John had written 'Day Tripper' (having a pop at what he referred to as 'weekend hippies'), while 'We Can Work It Out' (concerning Paul's troubled relationship with Jane Asher) was a joint Lennon-McCartney effort. It wasn't planned to have a double-A-side, more just a way of settling the argument as to which song should be prominent. Both are so good, this was the perfect solution.

1966

Nowhere Man/What Goes On

Released USA:	21 February 1966 on Capitol
UK:	Not released
USA:	3

The first 1966 offering released in the USA was, rather disappointingly, the first US single not to make it to No. 1 for over 18 months. Both tracks were taken from the Beatles' *Rubber Soul* album released for the Christmas market in 1965, strongly influenced by US folk, country and soul sounds they had enjoyed during their month on tour in America. Lennon wrote the folky 'Nowhere Man' about his own feelings of lacking personal direction. A nice song, with lovely three-part harmonies from John, Paul and George, but probably not the best choice as a single. Interestingly, the out-and-out country-and-western B-side, 'What Goes On', is the only Beatles song credited to Lennon-McCartney-Starkey.

Paperback Writer/Rain

Released UK:	10 June 1966 on Parlophone
Released USA:	30 May 1966 on Capitol
UK:	1
USA:	1

This was the point when the Beatles output – albums and singles – made a dramatic advance. Having been working at EMI Studios for several weeks on their next LP, *Revolver*, these two tracks didn't make it onto the album, but that's no reflection on their quality. The A-side, 'Paperback Writer', was a song McCartney penned when an aunt asked him why he only ever wrote songs about 'love'. Determined to prove her wrong, Paul came up with the idea of a song based on a letter written by an author to a book company asking them to consider publishing his book. On the B-side was Lennon's 'Rain' – the first Beatles record to use backward tapes and a much more prominent bass and drums sound. Ringo considers it his best drum recording. In addition, after three years of jangly Rickenbacker guitars, McCartney had been presented with a much bigger, longer, heavier and louder Rickenbacker bass, and the difference was instantly apparent. The best ever Beatles B-side? Many believe so, but it's up against a lot of competition.

Yellow Submarine/Eleanor Rigby

Released UK: 5 August 1966 on Parlophone
Released USA: 8 August 1966 on Capitol
UK: 1
USA: 2

Strange that the follow up single to 'Paperback Writer' should be released as another double-A-side, given that many dismiss 'Yellow Submarine' as a rather silly children's singalong, while 'Eleanor Rigby' is one of their finest ever recordings. But does it matter? There were some valid reasons to opt for the double-A-side. First, they were the Beatles; they could do whatever they wanted. Second, the animated movie *Yellow Submarine* had been released just the previous month, so it made perfect financial sense to bring out the theme song in support. It was specifically aimed at a young audience and it succeeded very well, both musically and filmicly. Not everyone loved it, but it was difficult to walk around British streets at the time without hearing children singing and adults whistling the theme tune. From happy… to despair. If 'Yellow Submarine' demonstrated the Beatles' experimental phase, 'Eleanor Rigby' went further still. McCartney wrote most of this sad, funerary masterpiece with lyrical assistance from his three colleagues. None of them played an instrument; Paul sang the lead vocals along with harmonies from Lennon and Harrison. It was then up to George Martin to produce a string arrangement for a string octet of violins, violas and cellos. Perfect. English baroque pop at its very finest.

THE BEATLES ON VINYL

1967

Strawberry Fields Forever/Penny Lane

Released UK:	17 February 1967 on Parlophone
Released USA:	13 February 1967 on Capitol
UK:	2
USA:	1

Just when you think things can't get any better, along comes 1967. The Beatles had returned to EMI Studios in December 1966 to work on what might prove to be their first concept album, based on the theme of their Liverpool childhoods. The first tune thrown into the hat was Lennon's 'Strawberry Fields Forever', referring to a Salvation Army children's home in Liverpool where he would play as a child. John had written the song while playing the role of Private Grimweed in the film *How I Won the War*, a black comedy directed by Dick Lester, who had been in charge of the Beatles' first two movies. With filming taking place in Almeria, Spain, over several weeks, Lennon often had a great deal of free time and spent it working on the song. George Martin recorded two versions – one with orchestration, the other with the full band at two different tempos. Not being able to make up his mind between the two, John asked George if he could combine them; it seemed impossible but, with help from sound engineer Geoff Emerick, they achieved it perfectly by speeding up one recording and slowing down the other. No-one expected it to work, but it did, and created the ephemeral, dreamy feel to the overall atmosphere.

Paul's response to John's superb demonstration of nostalgia was 'Penny Lane', a Liverpool district through which he would regularly travel on the bus on his way to and from school. LSD, once again, played a part in one of the Beatles' best-known and best-loved compositions. Paul's memories were compiled from actual locations either on or close to Penny Lane, including a barber's shop, fish 'n' chip shop and local fire station. He knew exactly the sound he wanted, which included what he described as a "tremendously high trumpet" that he'd heard on some TV show. Paul could play the trumpet a little bit as his father, Jim, was a decent player and had given him some lessons, but this was way beyond Paul's capabilities. George Martin hired David Mason – the musician Paul had heard on TV – to play a piccolo trumpet part so difficult that even he struggled, but eventually succeeded brilliantly.

So good were the recordings of 'Strawberry Fields Forever' and 'Penny Lane' that it was decided once again to release them as a double-A-side. Usually considered by worldwide polls to be the best ever Beatles single, remarkably it was the first one in the UK since 'Please Please Me' that didn't make it to No. 1. It remained hostage at No. 2 for 11 weeks thanks to Englebert Humperdinck's 'Release Me'. Such irony.

All You Need Is Love/Baby, You're a Rich Man

Released UK:	7 July 1967 on Parlophone
Released USA:	17 July 1967 on Capitol
UK:	1
USA:	1

With *Sgt. Pepper* finally finished and the Beatles riding high on a wave of worldwide success, the band were back in the studio obeying Brian Epstein's instructions to write a new song, with a simple but positive theme, to represent Great Britain on *Our World* – the world's first live, international satellite-television link, broadcast to around 500 million people across the globe. The outcome was John Lennon's 'All You Need Is Love' a sugar-coated, flower power, hippieland anthem reaching out to the global village to encourage us all to be… well, nicer to each another. In truth, it wasn't all quite as lovey-dovey as some of us remember. Some critics found the song a little naive and simplistic; others weren't impressed to discover that *Our World* wasn't entirely a live Beatles performance – some pre-recorded backing tapes were used; and sadly, as EMI discovered, love isn't all you need when another music publisher sues you for using a small segment of Glenn Miller's 'In the Mood' in the outro.

The B-side, 'Baby, You're A Rich Man' was a rather cynical snipe at the hippie movement, asking the question: "How does it feel to be one of the beautiful people?" Combining two different songs – one John's, the other Paul's – it works well and deserves to be better remembered than just because of its heavy use of a clavioline keyboard, a forerunner of the synthesiser. It was also the first Beatles song to be recorded at Olympic Sound Studios in Barnes, west London.

Hello, Goodbye/I Am the Walrus

Released UK:	24 November 1967 on Parlophone
Released USA:	27 November 1967 on Capitol
UK:	1
USA:	1

If ever there was a case for another double-A-sided record, this was it. 'Hello, Goodbye'/'I Am The Walrus' – Lennon's Lewis Carroll/Edward Lear-like gobbledegook masterpiece featuring weird lyrics, strange sound effects, backwards tape, upside-down tapes, extracts from a BBC Home Service broadcast of Shakespeare's *King Lear*... As Lennon happily admitted, virtually every line was written as a result of an LSD trip. It's a lot of trips. There are many who feel this is the best Beatles B-side and it's hard to disagree. Certainly it's the best B-side that should have been the A-side, but was considered totally bonkers and too risqué for the likes of a "pornographic priestess" to take the leading role. Lennon certainly wasn't happy to be told he'd been relegated to the B-side, but then he was up against another example of McCartney's brilliant baroque-esque pop, 'Hello, Goodbye'. As John commented to George Martin one day: "Let's face it, George, I don't expect to walk into a bar in Spain and hear people whistling 'I Am the Walrus'." But a double-A-side, whatever they say.

1968

Lady Madonna/The Inner Light (Harrison)

Released UK:	15 March 1968 on Parlophone
Released USA:	18 March 1968 on Capitol
UK:	1
USA:	4

Written by Paul on the piano and strongly influenced by the likes of Fats Domino and Fats Waller for their boogie-woogie, New Orleans-style of playing, this was the most straightforward Beatles A-side since 'Paperback Writer' over 18 months before. It's a great little blues-rocker with a memorable saxophone solo played by Ronnie Scott, famous, of course, as the proprietor of the legendary jazz club in his name located in London's Soho. When this single was released in March '68 the Beatles were visiting India to take part in a Transcendental Meditation study course under Maharishi Mahesh Yogi, which clearly had a lot to do with the B-side, 'The Inner Light'. This was the first time for a Beatles UK single to include a George Harrison composition, which was primarily recorded in Bombay. None of his bandmates featured on the instrumental backing, only backing vocals. The instruments were all played by Indian musicians under Harrison's direction. This was the last Beatles single to be released on Parlophone – it was Apple Records from this point on.

Hey Jude/Revolution

Released UK:	**30 August 1968 on Apple**
Released USA:	**26 August 1968 on Apple**
UK:	**1**
USA:	**1**

The first Beatles single on Apple was again written by Paul on the piano after paying a visit to Lennon's first wife, Cynthia, and their five-year-old son, Julian, following John's decision to leave his wife for Yoko Ono. 'Paul wrote the song to comfort Julian, which was originally titled 'Hey Jules', but later changed to 'Hey Jude' as Paul thought it sounded better. At over seven minutes long, this superb song (one of McCartney's best, which even Lennon begrudgingly agreed) concludes with its famous singalong ending – "Na, na-na, na-na-na-naaaaa", which Paul first played to test it out in the Oakley Arms, a pub in Bedfordshire. Unsurprisingly, it went down a storm. 'Hey Jude' was backed by a rare rocker from Lennon to reflect his support for social upheaval following political protesting, primarily against the war in Vietnam. He began writing the song during his trip to India when he was affected by media coverage of riots taking place across Europe and the USA. Two other versions of 'Revolution' were recorded at the same time and appeared on *The Beatles* 'White Album' – a slower blues version, 'Revolution 1' and the bizarre musical montage 'Revolution 9'.

1969

Get Back/Don't Let Me Down

Released UK:	11 April 1969 on Apple
Released USA:	5 May 1969 on Apple
UK:	1
USA:	1

As with 'Revolution', there are several different versions of 'Get Back'; this, the single, plus a different version for the *Let it Be* LP and others that appeared on various compilations. Early in '69 the band convened at Twickenham Film Studios to begin a TV documentary (which eventually became the motion picture *Let it Be*) preparing new songs for a live performance at the Roundhouse in north London. These became known as the 'Get Back' sessions, which eventually moved to their Apple Studios in London's Savile Row, where the famous rooftop gig took place. Penned by McCartney, with a rare guitar solo from Lennon, 'Get Back' is a great R&B number that demonstrated, no matter how deep were the internal problems being revealed within the documentary, the Beatles were still capable of producing some terrific music. Their friend and recent Apple Records signing, Billy Preston, plays keyboards both on 'Get Back' and the B-side, Lennon's soulful love song for Yoko. Such were Preston's contributions that the single was credited to 'The Beatles with Billy Preston' – the only external artist to be credited on a Beatles single.

The Ballad Of John and Yoko/Old Brown Shoe (Harrison)

Released UK:	30 May 1969 on Apple
Released USA:	17 July 1967 on Apple
UK:	1
USA:	8

'Get Back' was still at No. 1 when Lennon wrote and rush-released 'The Ballad Of John and Yoko', which bitter-humorously documented the couple's recent wedding in Gibraltar and honeymoon in Paris and Amsterdam (where their infamous week-long bed-in protest for peace had taken place at the Amsterdam Hilton). Despite Ringo being away filming the movie *The Magic Christian* with Peter Sellers, and George being out of the country, Lennon was keen to get the song recorded and released while his Amsterdam bedroom activities were still hot news and turned to Paul McCartney to help him out. Their internal wranglings were put to one side while John played acoustic and electric guitar (with some nice country licks throughout), and McCartney displayed his multi-instrumental skills once again playing piano, bass and drums. Not a lot was expected of 'The Ballad of John and Yoko' but it still made it to No. 1 in the UK. In America, however, it was less appreciated because of its lyrical references to 'Christ' and 'crucify me'. 'Old Brown Shoe' was Harrison's second single B-side contribution, a Dylanesque shuffle with a tremendous riff doubled up on bass and guitar by himself and McCartney. A decent record, but Harrison's moment of glory was just around the corner.

Something (Harrison)/Come Together

Released UK: **31 October 1969 on Apple**
Released USA: **6 October 1969 on Apple**
UK: **4**
USA: **1**

"The greatest love song of the past 50 years," said Frank Sinatra of 'Something', which is pretty cool, but a shame he initially attributed it to Lennon and McCartney. That must have hurt Harrison, but he got over it; this was his first Beatles A-side after all (although, once again, a double-A-sided single) which went on to become the second most covered Beatles song after McCartney's 'Yesterday' and regularly polls as one of the top 10 Beatles songs of all time. It's acknowledged that the other three Beatles agreed it was the best track on the album *Abbey Road*, as did producer George Martin who said, "It took my breath away," when he heard it for the first time. Harrison wrote the song on piano for his ex-wife Patti Boyd (she claims), although Harrison suggested it might not have been. More surprising is the fact that his finest achievement only made it to No. 4 in the UK charts as a result of it being listed as a double-A-side and that these were the two opening tracks on *Abbey Road*, which had already been available for over a month. Both deserved better. 'Come Together' is also rather brilliant: more Lennon gibberish plus McCartney's superb bass line and Harrison's delicate guitar solo – another standout track on one of the best albums of all time.

1970

Let It Be/You Know My Name (Look Up the Number)

Released UK:	6 March 1970 on Apple
Released USA:	11 March 1970 on Apple
UK:	2
USA:	1

As the collaboration and desire of the world's greatest band drew to a rather sad conclusion with each band member focussing on their own solo ambitions, how fitting that this movingly gospel single penned by McCartney should be their swansong. Based, according to McCartney, on a dream he had about his mother, Mary, who had sadly died of cancer in 1956, she visits him during the band's most tumultuous period and tells him: "It will be all right, just let it be." Mary McCartney proved correct in as much as the resulting single developing into something very all right, despite Lennon's lack of interest and his contribution to the recording not extending beyond backing vocals. 'Let it Be' remains one of the Beatles most popular songs and was used as the title for their final studio album released in 1970. On the album version, Lennon had handed over the LP's master tapes to the American producer Phil Spector, who added various different overdubs and much more orchestration. Most people prefer the single. John Lennon's final contribution to the Beatles' unsurpassed collection of singles was the B-side – a comical parody that swings from reggae to lounge-lizard easy listening through to the Goons, with no lyrics beyond the title plus some spoken ramblings from John. It had been recorded at Abbey Road studios back in 1967 (with a decent alto saxophone solo added by the Rolling Stones' Brian Jones) and completed in '69. It is quite funny and at least gave them all something to smile about as the final curtain descended.

The Long and Winding Road/For You Blue (Harrison)

Released USA:	11 May 1970 on Apple
UK:	Not released
USA:	1

Not quite the final curtain for the USA, as Apple released another of Paul's finest songs, 'The Long and Winding Road', written, somewhat incredibly for anyone other than Paul McCartney, on the same day as 'Let it Be' and taken from the album of the same name. Paul didn't intend 'The Long and Winding Road' ever to be a Beatles song and offered it to the likes of Tom Jones and Cilla Black. Both reluctantly turned it down for various reasons but did go on to record it (along with just about everybody else) a few years later. Given the circumstances of its release as the final Beatles single, it is a bit of a tear-jerker – or at least the original version minus Phil Spector's gushing orchestration is. Check out the version on the *Let it Be…Naked* album to hear it as McCartney intended. And pay attention to the bass line – one of the few occasions when Lennon is recorded playing bass on his Fender VI 6-string. On the B-side, 'For Your Blue' was another love song written by Harrison for his ex-wife Patti Boyd. Influenced by some time he'd spent in Woodstock with Bob Dylan and the Band, it's a nice country blues number with a lap-steel guitar solo from Lennon in the style of Elmore James. Harrison had never received his fair share of Beatles singles recordings, so only fitting that the very last B-side should be one of his compositions.

1995/96

Free As A Bird (Lennon)/Christmas Time (Is Here Again) (Lennon-McCartney-Harrison-Starkey)

Released UK:	4 December 1995 on Apple
Released USA:	4 December 1995 on Apple
UK:	2
USA:	6

Real Love (Lennon)/Baby's in Black

Released UK:	4 March 1996 on Apple
Released USA:	4 March 1996 on Apple
UK:	4
USA:	11

When, in 1995, Yoko Ono gave Paul McCartney a cassette of some of John's unfinished home demos recorded in their New York apartment, the remaining band members gathered at Paul's home studio in Peasmarsh, East Sussex, with ELO's Jeff Lynne as co-producer, to assess what could be made of them. The results were the first two new Beatles recordings since 1970, released as part of *The Beatles Anthology* project for a TV documentary plus a set of three double-albums and a lavish, large-format book. Not everyone was in favour of these two singles being released over 15 years after John Lennon's death, but both are decent songs that have been recreated tastefully and touchingly by his former bandmates. The B-sides are also of valid interest – the Christmas song being recorded for their fan club back in 1967 and the only track on a Beatles single credited to all four band members. And 'Baby's in Black' is a live recording from the famous Hollywood Bowl concert back in 1965.

SINGLES BOXSETS

The 24 UK and 33 US original Beatles 7-inch singles aren't too difficult to track down at reasonable prices at secondhand record stores, record fairs or online, but various Beatles singles boxsets are also available.

THE SINGLES COLLECTION (1962-1970)

Released by Parlophone on 5 March 1976, this collection contains all 22 UK singles available at the time plus a new addition – Yesterday/I Should Have Know Better. All of the singles were available to buy individually or with the option of a cardboard storage box included for those who bought all 23 singles together.

THE BEATLES COLLECTION (1962-1978)

This later version of the above was originally released in 1976 by EMI's subsidiary World Records for international buyers by mail-order only. It included the 23 singles as above plus one more: Back in the U.S.S.R./Twist and Shout which had been released by Parlophone in 1976 and made it to No. 19 in the UK charts. Later versions of the boxset added a double-single released in the UK and USA in 1978 which coupled Sgt. Pepper's Lonely Hearts Club Band and With a Little Help From My Friends, plus an additional one-sided single of A Day in the Life. It made it to No. 63 in the UK and No. 71 in the US.

THE BEATLES RSD BOXSET

Released by Apple and Capitol in 2011 primarily for the US market as part of the international annual Record Store Day, this re-mastered boxset includes four US singles in their original artwork: Ticket to Ride/Yes it Is; Yellow Submarine/Eleanor Rigby; Hey Jude/Revolution; and Something/Come Together. Why those four singles were chosen is anyone's guess, but the boxset is still fairly easy to find online in the US and UK.

THE SINGLES COLLECTION

Released by Apple in 2019, this latest boxset includes all of the UK singles plus Free as a Bird and Real Love as a new double-A-sided single. All UK singles are included in a variety of picture sleeves of releases from around the world. The collection is readily available and not outrageously expensive for what is arguably the greatest collection of singles ever recorded. Treat yourself.

SINGLES

EPs (EXTENDED PLAY)

Twist and Shout

Tracks:	**Twist and Shout/A Taste of Honey/Do You Want to Know a Secret/There's a Place**
Released:	**12 July 1963**
Label:	**Parlophone**
UK:	**1**
USA:	**Not released**

The first Beatles EP remains the biggest selling EP in UK history. With sales of over 800,000 copies, it remained in the charts for 64 weeks – 21 weeks at No. 1. All four tracks were taken from their debut album *Please Please Me*, with only Side 2 featuring Lennon-McCartney compositions. The wonderful cover image was taken by the photographer Fiona Adams on a London wartime bombsite near Euston Square tube station.

The Beatles' Hits

Tracks:	**From Me to You/Thank You Girl/Please Please Me/Love Me Do**
Released:	**6 September 1963**
Label:	**Parlophone**
UK:	**1**
USA:	**Not released**

The second EP arrived less than two months after Twist and Shout and also made it straight to No. 1 for three weeks, remaining in the charts for 43 weeks. Cover image by Angus McBean (from the same session for the Please Please Me album cover in February that year) with sleeve notes from Tony Barrow.

The Beatles No. 1

Tracks:	**I Saw Her Standing There/Misery/Anna (Go to Him)/Chains**
Released:	**1 November 1963**
Label:	**Parlophone**
UK:	**2**
USA:	**Not released**

Once again it was less than two months before the third Beatles EP arrived. It stayed in the charts for 29 weeks, but only made it as high as No. 2. Cover image again taken from Angus McBean's *Please Please Me* cover shoot.

All My Loving

Tracks:	All My Loving/Ask Me Why/Money (That's What I Want/P.S. I Love You
Released:	7 February 1964
Label:	Parlophone
UK:	1
USA:	Not released

The fourth EP comprised of two tracks from the *With the Beatles* LP released in November the previous year (re-using Robert Freeman's moody album cover image), plus two more songs once again from *Please Please Me*. This added up to 12 of the 14 songs from their debut album having now been re-released on EPs.

Souvenir of their Visit to USA

Tracks:	Misery/A Taste of Honey/Ask Me Why/Anna (Go to Him)
Released:	23 March 1964
Label:	Vee-Jay
UK:	Not released
USA:	Did not chart

EPs have never been very popular in the USA and this was the first of only three to be released. The latter two didn't sell very well at all but this one was a great success because Vee-Jay offered it as a mail-order purchase. That decision meant, however, that the Billboard Hot 100 would not recognize the sales, so it did not chart.

Four by the Beatles

Tracks:	**Roll Over Beethoven/All My Loving/This Boy/Please Mr. Postman**
Released:	**11 May 1964**
Label:	**Capitol**
UK:	**Not released**
USA:	**92**

The first EP release from Capitol was their response to Vee-Jay's success, using four songs that Capitol had previously released as singles in Canada, both selling very well. US sales, however, were disappointing and it only just crawled into the Top 100.

Long Tall Sally

Tracks:	**Long Tall Sally/I Call Your Name/Slow Down/Matchbox**
Released:	**19 June 1964**
Label:	**Parlophone**
UK:	**1**
USA:	**Not released**

The fifth UK Beatles EP release featured four tracks, none of which had already appeared in the UK as singles or on either of their first two albums. All four were used by Capitol over in the USA as album tracks. Another excellent black and white image from Robert Freeman on the cover, while, for the first time, the Beatles' press officer, Derek Taylor, wrote the sleeve notes.

A Hard Day's Night (Extracts From the Film)

Tracks:	**I Should Have Known Better/If I Fell/Tell Me Why/And I Love Her**
Released:	**4 November 1964**
Label:	**Parlophone**
UK:	**1**
USA:	**Not released**

A Hard Day's Night (Extracts From the Album)

Tracks :	**Any Time at All/I'll Cry Instead/Things We Said Today/When I Get Home**
Released:	**6 November 1964**
Label:	**Parlophone**
UK:	**8**
USA:	**Not released**

An unusual sales pitch from Parlophone, releasing two EPs two days apart with four tracks taken from the film *A Hard Day's Night* but eight in total from the album of the same name, both of which had been released four months earlier in July. Explains, sort of, why the Extracts From the Film EP sold better than the other, because fans wanted a souvenir of the film, but not eight tracks from an album many of them already owned. Robert Freeman's iconic album cover images are used on both EPs.

4 by the Beatles

Released:	**1 February 1965**
Tracks:	**Honey Don't/I'm a Loser/Mr. Moonlight/Everybody's Trying to Be My Baby**
Label:	**Capitol**
UK:	**Not released**
USA:	**68**

Might not seem a very creative title from Capitol, given that the company's first Beatles EP had the same name, but this was inspired by that original record to create a '4-By' series of EPs for a number of bands. In the end, only the Beach Boys and the Beatles released '4-By' EPs before the project was dropped. The four tracks were taken from the *Beatles '65* album and included two Carl Perkins numbers and Roy Lee Johnson's 'Mr. Moonlight'.

Beatles for Sale

Tracks:	**No Reply/I'm a Loser/Rock and Roll Music/Eight Days a Week**
Released:	**6 April 1965**
Label:	**Parlophone**
UK:	**1**
USA:	**Not released**

The Beatles' eighth EP with four tracks taken from the album of the same name released the previous December. Made it to No. 1 twice for a total of six weeks at the top spot. Robert Freeman's distinctive album cover image was used again for the EP, with sleeve notes from Tony Barrow.

Beatles for Sale No. 2

Tracks:	**I'll Follow the Sun/Baby's in Black/Words of Love/I Don't Want to Spoil the Party**
Released:	**4 June 1965**
Label:	**Parlophone**
UK:	**5**
USA:	**Not released**

The second Beatles for Sale EP arrived just two months later with four more tracks from the hugely successful LP of the same name, including Buddy Holly's 'Words of Love'. Another excellent Robert Freeman front cover shot and no sleeve notes other than a list of the eight previous Beatles EPs.

The Beatles' Million Sellers

Tracks:	**She Loves You/I Want to Hold Your Hand/Can't Buy Me Love/I Feel Fine**
Released:	**6 December 1965**
Label:	**Parlophone**
UK:	**1**
USA:	**Not released**

As it says on the tin, this was an EP release featuring Beatles singles that had each sold over one million copies. Here were a few more pennies to add to the Beatles' magic money tree, making it to No.1 for four weeks. No sleeve notes apart from a list of eight previous EPs (not including Long Tall Sally for some reason) but a front cover image from a new name – photographer Robert Whitaker.

Yesterday

Tracks:	**Yesterday/Act Naturally/You Like Me Too Much/It's Only Love**
Released:	**4 March 1966**
Label:	**Parlophone**
UK:	**1**
USA:	**Not released**

The Beatles' 11th EP unsurprisingly made it to No. 1 virtually immediately, held the position for six weeks and remained in the charts for a further seven weeks largely due to the fact that 'Yesterday' hadn't been released as a single in the UK, despite its huge popularity. The four Lennon-McCartney songs were featured on the Beatles' soundtrack album accompanying their second movie, *Help!*, with lead vocals shared between each band member. Another standout front cover shot from Robert Whitaker and the full list of previous EPs with Long Tall Sally making a return.

Nowhere Man

Tracks:	**Nowhere Man/Drive My Car/Michelle/You Won't See Me**
Released:	**8 July 1966**
Label:	**Parlophone**
UK:	**4**
USA:	**Not released**

Four more Lennon-McCartney tracks for the Beatles' penultimate EP, all taken from the band's most recent album, *Rubber Soul*, released over seven months previously. That probably explains why it only made it to No. 4 in the UK charts, despite four great songs from their transitional album that initiated the Beatles conversion from poppers into virtual proggers. Robert Freeman had taken *Rubber Soul*'s famous front cover shot but it was a Robert Whitaker image selected once again for the related EP, taken in London's Chiswick Park.

Magical Mystery Tour

Tracks:

Record 1:	Magical Mystery Tour/Your Mother Should Know/I Am the Walrus.
Record 2:	The Fool on the Hill/Flying/Blue Jay Way
Released:	8 December 1967
Label:	Parlophone
UK:	2
USA:	Not released

By the time *Magical Mystery Tour* was released in December 1967 it had been 17 months since the Beatles' previous EP, signaling a reduction in the sales of extended play records as albums became increasingly more important. It's unlikely that the Beatles would have released another one if it hadn't been for the TV movie project, *Magical Mystery Tour*, accompanied by the UK's first double-EP, which was kept off the No. 1 spot only by their own single 'Hello, Goodbye'. There were too many tracks for a single-disc EP, but not enough for an album (although, as usual, Capitol Records disagreed and simply added another five non-album singles, much to the band's disappointment). This was a rather special release: it's the first Beatles EP available in mono or stereo and comes with a 32-page, mind-blowingly colourful booklet containing the lyrics, movie stills, cast list and a graphic novella-style comic book designed by Beatle Book cartoonist Bob Gibson, all forming one element of a decidedly wacky, LSD-induced, psychedelic road trip. When the TV film was broadcast by the BBC on Boxing Day 1967, it didn't help that something so colourful was shown in black and white, as colour TV wasn't yet readily available! Truth is, black and white or colour, the music is sublime; the TV film is not.

THE BEATLES EP COLLECTION

Released by Parlophone in 1981 containing all 13 Beatles EPs with one addition, *The Beatles*, featuring previously unavailable stereo mixes of four songs: The Inner Light; Baby, You're a Rich Man; She's a Woman; and This Boy. This EP collection is not too difficult to find online or at record fairs but is likely to cost you £200+. There's also a Japanese red vinyl edition available for considerably more.

THE BEATLES ON VINYL

BEATLES TOP 20 ALBUMS

Based on a wide range of international sales figures (some certified, some estimated), the Beatles are without doubt the most successful artists in the world with higher sales than second-placed Elvis Presley and third-placed Michael Jackson. Sales figures are very difficult to confirm and have fluctuated considerably over the last 20 years with the addition of streaming and downloading, but no statistical organisations have challenged the Beatles' status as the toppermost of the poppermost. Estimated actual (rather than certified) worldwide sales of Beatles albums are in the region of 600+ million.

Either way, sales figures are one thing, but which of the Beatles albums are the most popular around the world? Calculated on international voting statistics in more than 40,000 of the world's 'best ever albums' polls, the Beatles LPs (based on original countries of release but not including compilations or boxsets) are ranked at the time of going to press in 2021 as follows:

BEATLES TOP 20 ALBUMS

20. The Beatles VI (US)
19. The Beatles at the Hollywood Bowl (UK/US)
18. The Beatles Second Album (US)
17. Beatles '65 (US)
16. Yesterday and Today (US)
15. Yellow Submarine (UK/US)
14. Meet the Beatles (US)
13. Let it Be... Naked (UK/US)
12. With the Beatles (UK)
11. Beatles For Sale (UK)
10. Please Please Me (UK)
9. A Hard Day's Night (UK)
8. Help! (UK)
7. Let it Be (UK/US)
6. Magical Mystery Tour (US)
5. Rubber Soul (UK)
4. The Beatles ('White Album') (UK/US)
3. Sgt. Pepper's Lonely Hearts Club Band (UK/US)
2. Revolver (UK)
1. Abbey Road (UK/US)

ACKNOWLEDGEMENTS AND SOURCES

"There are only four people who knew what the Beatles were about anyway."
Sir Paul McCartney MBE

There are thousands of Beatles titles out there but the following books, periodicals, films and websites have provided invaluable in-depth information and quotations. All are highly recommended:

Babiuk, Andy	*Beatles Gear*
Bacon, Tony & Morgan, Gareth	*Paul McCartney: Playing the Great Beatles Basslines*
Beatles, The	*The Beatles Anthology*
Braun, Michael	*Love Me Do: The Beatles' Progress*
Burrows, Terry	*The Art of Sound: A Visual History for Audiophiles*
Carr, Roy	*Beatles at the Movies*
Coleman, Ray	*Lennon: The Definitive Biography*
Coleman, Ray	*Brian Epstein: The Man Who Made the Beatles*
Davies, Hunter	*The Beatles: The Authorised Biography*
DiLello, Richard	*The Longest Cocktail Party*
Emerick, Geoff & Massey, Howard	*Here, There and Everywhere: My Life Recording the Music of the Beatles*
Epstein, Brian	*A Cellarful of Noise*
Freeman, Robert	*Yesterday: Photographs of the Beatles*
Hayward, Mark	*The Beatles on Camera, Off Guard*
Hill, Tim & Clayton, Marie (Compilers)	*The Beatles Unseen Archives*
Hoffmann, Dezo	*The Beatles Conquer America*
Howlett, Kevin	*The Beatles in Mono*
Lewisohn, Mark	*The Complete Beatles Chronicle*
MacDonald, Ian	*Revolution in the Head: The Beatles' Records and the Sixties*
MacDonald, Ian	*The People's Music*
McCabe, Peter & Schonfeld, Robert D.	*Apple to the Core: The Unmaking of the Beatles*
Martin, George	*All You Need is Ears*
Miles, Barry	*Paul McCartney: Many Years From Now*
Miles, Barry	*The British Invasion*
Miles, Barry	*Hippie*
Norman, Philip	*Shout! The Beatles in Their Generation*
Norman, Philip	*John Lennon: The Life*
Norman, Philip	*Paul McCartney: The Biography*
Palmer, Tony	*All You Need is Love: The Story of Popular Music*

ACKNOWLEDGEMENTS AND SOURCES

Roberts, David (Editor)	*Guinness British Hit Singles*
Starr, Ringo	*Postcards from the Boys*
Wenner, Jann	*Lennon Remembers*
Williams, Allan & Marshall, William	*The Man Who Gave the Beatles Away*
Womack, Kenneth	*Maximum Volume: The Life of Beatles Producer George Martin. The Early Years 1926-1966*
Womack, Kenneth	*Sound Pictures: The Life of Beatles Producer George Martin. The Later Years 1966-2016*

Newspapers

Daily Mail (London)
Daily Mirror (London)
Daily Telegraph (London)
Guardian (London)
Independent (London)
New York Times
Sunday Times (London)
Times (London)

Periodicals

Billboard
Long Live Vinyl
Magnet
Melody Maker
Mojo
New Musical Express
Q
Record Mirror
Record Collector
Rolling Stone
Sunday Times Magazine
Uncut

Television/video/DVD

A Geezer & A Blonde Productions, London 2017 – **It was Fifty Years Ago Today! The Beatles: Sgt. Pepper and Beyond**

Apple Corps/BBC 1967 – **Magical Mystery Tour**

Apple Corps 1970 – **Let it Be**

Apple Corps/EMI Records/ITV 1995 – **The Beatles Anthology**

Apple Corps/StudioCanal/PolyGram Entertainment 2016 – **Eight Days A Week: The Touring Years**

BBC Arena/Grounded Productions/Eagle Rock Entertainment 2011 – **Produced by George Martin**

Commonwealth United Corporation 1969 – **The Magic Christian** (Peter Sellers/Ringo Starr)

HBO 2011 **George Harrison: Living in the Material World**

London Weekend Television/Isolde Films/Tony Palmer 1977 (TV)/2008 (DVD) – **All You Need is Love: The Story of Popular Music**

Prism Films 2011 – **Strange Fruit: The Beatles' Apple Records**

United Artists 1964 – **A Hard Day's Night**

United Artists 1965 – **Help!**

United Artists 1967 – **How I Won the War** (Michael Crawford/John Lennon)

United Artists 1968 – **Yellow Submarine**

Web sites

albumlinernotes.com

allmusic.com

beatlesbible.com

beatlesbooks.com

beatlesdiscs.blogspot.com

beatleswiki.com

billboard.com

discogs.com

longlivevinyl.net

magnetmagazine.com

mojo4music.com

nme.com

qthemusic.com

recordcollectormag.com

rockcellarmagazine.com

rollingstone.com

teamrock.com

ultimateclassicrock.com

uncut.co.uk

webgrafikk.com (The Daily Beatle)

Pete Chrisp has worked as a writer and editor for newspapers, magazines and books since 1979. His books include the highly acclaimed *Riding Shotgun*, co-written with Rory Gallagher's bass player Gerry McAvoy, and best-selling *The Chain: 50 Years of Fleetwood Mac*. He has also edited myriad music books across a wide range of topics – from the Byrds and folk music through to tube amps and collectable guitars. He lives in Kent, England

For their help, advice and encouragement, many thanks to Gary O'Neill, Huw Thomas, Carolyn McHugh, Sally Beeby and Trish Coveney.

In memory of Ringo's stunt double: Mick Dillon, 1926-2006.

And for the next generation of Beatles F.A.N.s – Flo, Archie and Nina.

"You expect people our age to know the music but actually a lot of kids know the music and if anything is left, we have left really good music and that's the important part."

Sir Richard Starkey MBE

ACKNOWLEDGEMENTS AND SOURCES